H●MEM▲KERS

wm

WILLIAM MORROW

An Imprint of HarperCollins*Publishers*

A DOMESTIC HANDBOOK FOR THE DIGITAL GENERATION

HOMEMAKERS

BRIT
MORIN

founder and CEO of **BRIT+CO**

This book is written as a source of information only. The information contained in this book should by no means be considered a substitute for the advice, decision, or judgment of the reader's physician or other professional adviser.

All efforts have been made to ensure the accuracy of the information contained in this book as of the date published. The author and the publisher expressly disclaim responsibility for any adverse effects arising from the use or application of the information contained herein.

HarperCollins books may be purchased for educational, business, or sales promotional use. For information please e-mail the Special Markets Department at SPsales@harpercollins.com.

Brit + Co Credits:
Creative Director: Anjelika Temple
Designer: Annie Kubena
Photographer: Chris Andre
Illustrator: Nate Koehler Illustration
Food Production: Sarah Jones
DIY Production: Roxanne Taghavian and Kelly Bryden
Stylist: Misty Spinney

FIRST EDITION

Interior Text Design Layout by Diahann Sturge

Library of Congress Cataloging-in-Publication Data has been applied for.

ISBN 978-0-06-233250-9

15 16 17 18 19   OV/RRD   10 9 8 7 6 5 4 3 2 1

*

*To the men and women in my life who have taught me
to be strong, courageous, and ambitious enough to
build a career outside the home, and for my husband
Dave, son Ansel, and dog Pixel, who have inspired me
to build a beautiful life inside it as well.*

*

CONTENTS

HOMEMAKERS

ENTRYWAY

I never wanted to write a book.

After all, I come from the digital generation. You know, the generation that prefers Instagram to Kodak cameras and can't focus on anything for longer than two minutes. The generation of which 72% downloaded at least one app in the past week. Yes, that generation.

So let me explain why you're now reading this. I'll start from the beginning.

I've always had a very strong drive simply to create. When I was a year old, I was building with blocks. By two, I couldn't put down my crayons and markers. And don't even get me started on finger paint. A few years later, I was making up stories about my stuffed animals, decorating and redecorating (and re-redecorating) my room, and teaching myself to French-braid my own hair.

As a teenager, I started experimenting with sewing machines, ovens, and power tools. My mom (awesomely) let me have a cell phone at age thirteen. I used my computer to write short stories and to play Oregon Trail. I forded many rivers back in those days.

And then the Internet happened.

By the time I was legally able to drink, I was a full-on tech nerd. I spent most of my college life working remotely for Silicon Valley companies. I scored a gig at Apple, learned how to code, and then transitioned to a career at Google. And I loved my job. I worked at the number one "best place to work" in the country. What was not to love?

Well, for one thing, working in tech meant spending endless hours at my desk and online—eating via takeout, doing all my holiday shopping on Amazon, and hiring people to do such mundane real-world things as hanging a coat rack. Staring at that big (then increasingly small) screen all day, day after day, took the idea of "living in the cloud" to a whole new level.

Then something changed. I left my job at Google to start a tech company of my own, but first I decided to give myself a break. Those six months may have been the most transformative of my life.

They say you should try to make your hobby your career, but I didn't even know what my hobby was. So I chose not to schedule myself at all and to see what I naturally gravitated toward each day.

I ended up deciding that what I really wanted to do was learn how to do and make new things. I joined a "makerspace" called TechShop, which is basically a gym for making things. After paying a hundred bucks or so a month, you can come in whenever you want and use all of their machines. And, man, do they have some incredible machines! Sewing machines, 3D printers, laser cutters, wood saws, screen printers . . . the list goes on and on.

I learned how to design things in 3D, how to laser-cut wood (and even vegetables) and more. During this same period, I took all kinds of advanced cooking and baking classes. I even got certified in letterpress printing. My favorite part was learning how to create my own polymer plates online, which saved me tons of time working with the press.

All the while, I was also continuing to experiment with creating software. I used new online applications that helped me brush up on my coding skills, and I even programmed a few little apps of my own.

Turns out, my favorite hobby was (and still is) creating. It didn't matter what I was working on, as long as I was making something. On an average day, I'd make a terrarium in the morning, 3D-print a necklace by noon, spend my post-siesta time coding, paint a canvas by sunset, and end the day with homemade ice cream.

The beauty in all this was that whether I was designing a 3D necklace on my computer to print in real life, using apps that taught me how to letterpress, or scouring the web for delicious recipes to re-create, I was naturally using the virtual world to help me make stuff in the physical one.

That's the lightbulb that clicked on in my head: today's generation thrives in the virtual world, but as humans we remain inspired to work and create in the physical world. Why can't these two worlds come together?

Turns out, they can.

(Now comes the part where I decided to write a book.)

Not unlike many peers of mine, I consume a *lot* of information online. And while many argue that we will soon face the end of books and magazines, digital media seems to be having an ironic opposite effect: the value of an analog piece of work is much higher than its digital counterpart. In fact, sales of printed books are *up* year over year! In today's Internet era, analog works of creativity are treated more like art and less like links you can toss around to your five thousand Facebook friends. These projects are touched by your hands, displayed on your walls, and saved for years on end. And depending on the subject matter, they may be referenced hundreds of times and may even be passed down from one generation to the next.

After thinking long and hard about this book-writing project, I realized that the internal challenge I was facing in writing a book was basically a metaphor for how I see my generation these days.

"To make something, with my own hands—it's something our generation wasn't taught, and it's so empowering. You can feel a zeitgeist around this."
INTERVIEW, *SAN FRANCISCO CHRONICLE,* 2012

We have spent the past decade so immersed in the digital world that our bodies are aching to participate in real, physical human experiences we can create in the analog world. Some are even paying to attend "digital detox" camps just to get away from their virtual reality.

"Forty-two percent of Gen X and Gen Y say that moments that aren't documented are 'wasted.'"

It is for these reasons that I started my company, Brit + Co. There's a movement afoot that celebrates creativity by balancing the digital and the analog, but this movement needs a new generation of teachers—people who grew up like me, with the benefit of all the efficiencies that modern technology has to offer, but who have stayed true to their "maker" and human roots. Brit + Co helps adults unlock their creativity and rediscover their inner child— the one who used to love to draw, build, and play. We believe that every human being is an artist and that every moment of our lives is a canvas. Our homes are our grounding place, the space where we are both extroverts and introverts, where we relax as much as we work. Shouldn't creativity begin there?

WHAT IS THIS BOOK?

This is neither your grandma's guidebook nor your home economics teacher's textbook (assuming, of course, you ever took home ec). In fact, this book challenges the idea that there's still such a thing as a "homemaker" at all.

The rules of homemaking have changed, and this book is here to serve as your new guide for creative living, both in and out of the home. I'll walk you through each room of the house, catching you up on all the basic "must-know" skills you may have missed, sharing technologies that can help you save time and be more creative, and also showing you easy DIY projects you can complete. Before we leave each room, I'll give you a foreshadowing of what the future looks like for that part of the home. (Spoiler alert: there are some crazy cool new technologies coming your way that will make it even easier to be creative.) As you come to understand how your role as "homemaker" may evolve to "home maker," prepare to have your mind blown—this stuff could be real in the next few years.

Follow along as we tour the modern home, discuss its larger meaning in our world, and learn how to live a simpler and more creative life, all while taking a step further into the digital age.

HOMEMAKERS: PAST AND PRESENT

My mom 1986

What is a homemaker these days? A term that was first used in 1876, "homemaker" is defined in the dictionary as "one who manages a household, especially a wife or mother."

For my grandmother's generation (the 1930s to the 1960s), that was exactly what the term meant. At the end of the Second World War, only 10% of married women with children under the age of six held a job or were seeking a job. The rest stayed at home. Back in the mid-twentieth century, "homemaker" largely referred to a woman who was unemployed and spent her days cooking, cleaning, and taking care of the kids and the home. A famous adage of *Ladies' Homemaker Monthly,* a preeminent homemaker's journal at the time, declared: "You can judge a good woman by how many well-dressed children she has and the contentment of her husband." *Good Housekeeping* was also very popular in this period. In fact, it was Hearst Corporation's most profitable monthly magazine back then. Its best-selling book, *Guide for Young Homemakers* (1966), includes what many today would say are ludicrous instructions for women:

Personal grooming for health as well as good looks concerns the modern housewife as a practical matter. She must budget her time for it, shop wisely for cosmetics and beauty aids, and learn to use them for best results. She may find herself in the role of counselor to a growing daughter. Above all, a sensible regard for her everyday appearance contributes to a happy home. A lovely wife pleases husband and children, favorably impresses guests, and faces the outside world with confidence.

No matter how many experts you consult, you still have to brush
your hair, cream your skin, coddle your hands. You have to exercise
and diet, stand and move like a beauty. No one else can do these
things for you. In daily housekeeping, care of the figure is perhaps the
beautifying measure most overlooked.

Excuse me while I go throw up now.

Among my mother's generation (the 1970s to the 1990s), nearly half of all women worked, and a majority of them were young mothers taking care of kids like me. In fact, in 1985, the year I was born, the participation in the workforce of women between the ages of 25 and 44 soared to 71%, a tripling of the numbers from 1950. This also happened to be the start of the infamous pantsuits and shoulder pads trend for women. (Yikes, what a trend that was.) Gone were the days when most women aspired to wear A-line dresses and aprons; these women were now in the workforce trying to look the part to fit in with their male colleagues.

Today the American family has changed yet again. Only one in five families have a stay-at-home mom and working dad. On the flip side, one in five families has a stay-at-home dad and working mom. This figure has doubled in the past 25 years.

More than ever before, women are becoming the breadwinners in their household. Over 40% of moms are now the sole or primary source of income, and those working at the same time as their spouse bring home 44% of their family's total income.

Because of a decrease in marriage and high divorce rates, single-parent families are an abundant reality of today's generation, meaning that women must learn how to take charge both at home and at work. Today nearly 60% of all women are employed, with more than 75% of women ages 25 to 44 participating in the labor force. Great progress, ladies, but just because you're now running the office doesn't mean you've gotten off the hook of running the home.

THE NEW WORKFORCE

Share of mothers who are breadwinners or co-breadwinners, 1967 to 2008

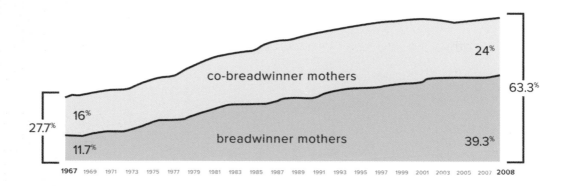

Heather Boushey and Jeff Chapman's analysis of Miriam King, Steven Ruggles, Trent Alexander, Donna Leicach, and Matthew Sobek. Integrated Public Use Microdata Series, Current Population Survey: Version 2.0. (Machine-readable database) Minneapolis, MN: Minnesota Population Center (producer and distributor), 2009.

NOTES: Breadwinner mothers include single mothers who work and married mothers who earn as much as or more than their husbands. Co-breadwinners are wives who bring home at least 25% of the couple's earnings, but less than half. The data only include families with a mother who is between the ages of 18 and 60 and who has children under age 18 living with her.

These days, Ward Cleaver wouldn't be able to afford a house in the suburbs or Beaver's tuition—unless June went to work too.

NICHOLAS KULISH, *NEW YORK TIMES,* SEPTEMBER 23, 2005

Q: Do you agree or disagree: Compared to your father, you are more comfortable having women work outside the home?

Agree: 70%

Disagree: 23%

Source: Rockefeller/*Time* poll, 2009

Some good news is that men's attitudes about women's ability to balance work and family have also shifted in a positive direction. In 1977, fewer than half of all men (49%) agreed with the statement "A mother who works outside the home can have just as good a relationship with her children as a mother who does not work." Thirty years later—a short time in terms of attitude shifts—two-thirds of men agreed with that statement (as did 80% of women). And the younger the respondent, the more pronounced this shift in attitude.

Turns out, many men today can also be described as homemakers, though they are still doing less housework than their female counterparts. While there's still a significant gap on this score between men and women, it's nice to see men contributing more often. And might I also give major props to the women who are working full-time jobs and *still* doing 28 hours of household work per week? It's no wonder they call you Super Woman.

The most recent figures from the National Survey of Families and Households at the University of Wisconsin show that husbands are doing about 14 hours of housework per week, compared with 31 hours for stay-at-home wives. But when both husband and wife work full-time outside the home, the wife does 28 hours and the husband does 16.

Perhaps more interesting is the fact that today's working women are also more comfortable in their own skin, opting to dress more fashionably at work even if that puts them at odds with the pantsuit past. Unlike the generation before them, this is a group of women with big career ambitions, yet they also care about having a beautiful and presentable home. In short, we want it all: to be the CEO and the homemaker, even though many women these days don't identify as such.

When I asked my own social media following to define "homemaker" today, their responses were mixed:

While the concept is very much intact, I think the term "homemaker" is a bit antiquated. To me (and I am at home full-time myself) the term limits the role of the mom. It doesn't make room for how she can run the home and generate income from the same space. I prefer "work-at-home mom" or "home manager."

DENEDRIANE DEAN

Although our definition of the word "homemaker" has changed vastly over time, our definition of the word "home" has not. Our home is our refuge, our safe place, the little piece of the world that is ours. Homemaking today isn't just about domestication and fancy dinner parties, although it certainly can be, it's about creating our space. Literally making our house (or apartment, tent, or Airstream trailer) into the place we can't wait to get back to at the end of the day or out-of-town trip. Homemaking is about filling your space with things and people you love. And the best part is the uniqueness of that concept. Your home is yours to make.

CELESTE KING

My home is where I retreat to relax, to celebrate with close friends, and most importantly, where I create. I work from home as the Director of Events for a food+tech startup, and I love being able to step away from my desktop to make a batch of strawberry jam, water the heirloom tomatoes I'm growing, or to continue adding personal touches to our comic-book-themed living room. I wouldn't trade this sort of freedom for the world!

VERA DEVERA

Being called a homemaker is a compliment, ladies! It means we know how to keep our families well fed, well clothed, and happy—and look good doing it. We can bake cookies, make our own laundry soap, and make our husband's day by having a delicious meal waiting for him. Let the men conquer the world. Ladies, we've got more important things to do. [Note from Brit: Hmmm . . .]

ANDREA GRAY

Being a "homemaker" means that you complete all household chores, run all necessary errands, and if you have kids, take them everywhere they have to go, leaving plenty of time for you to have dinner on the table the moment your husband swings open the door and proclaims/half sings, "Honey! I'm home!" I'm kidding, of course! In today's world, "homemaker," contrary to the 1950s term, doesn't apply solely to women, but to people who strive to make their homes and daily lives more colorful, healthy, organized, and, dare I say, exciting!

STEPHANIE PISANO

Young women today don't have the basic skill set their mothers did. And proper tech etiquette (like how to keep a clean inbox) should be seamlessly incorporated into the rest of homemaking advice.

REDEFINING THE HOMEMAKER TITLE

It's clear that we may be ready for a new definition of this old-fashioned word.

This is a special time in history. As already mentioned, it's the first time a generation has grown up with technology like the Internet. They call us "digital natives," a term that apparently refers to anyone born from 1980 on. I will add that you are *especially* a part of this group if you: (a) remember your first AIM profile name, (b) had a cell phone as a teenager, and (c) refer to Oregon Trail as a "childhood classic." Others might call us Millennials.

What's interesting about this sector of society is not just that there are a lot of us—80 million in the US alone, in fact, thanks to our 40 million parents, the Baby Boomers—but that we are all connected and highly educated, yet lack many of the skills that our moms and grandmas (and grandmas' grandmas) took for granted while growing up. Learning skills like sewing, cooking, and woodworking was not part of our academic challenges. If any of us had access to a home economics or shop class, it was probably an elective subject that we could opt into but weren't forced to take. From my own experience, I can not-so-proudly state that I did choose to take a semester of home ec in high school, but all I can remember making were basic chocolate chip cookies. And we baked them as a group of six, not on our own. Not exactly an in-depth domestic learning experience, if you ask me.

Couple our lack of domestic skills with the fact that our moms were the first in the "working women" generation, and you'll begin to understand why so many of us are now slightly freaking out over the idea of having to host a dinner party, decorate a living room, or build furniture. We were not taught domestic skills like our mothers were because our mothers were not around as often to teach them to us. While they were at work, trying to change the status quo of women in professional jobs, we were at home, toying with our computers instead of learning how to make dinner.

To further prove my case, take a look at something a Brit + Co reader recently wrote to me:

My mom was named Miss Betty Crocker of Springfield, New Jersey, in 1967. Thirty-five years later, I graduated from an all-girls high school that scorned home-ec class as "sexist." Though I could speak Spanish, recite from The Canterbury Tales, *and figure out the volume of a cone, I couldn't do laundry, change a tire, or sew on a button. I was educated, but fairly dumb. Since then I've taken it upon myself to learn the DIY skills I'd missed out on.*

Countless women I've interviewed have confided that they don't know how to use their oven, put up wallpaper, or fold their sheets the proper way. (I'll be honest and admit that I too didn't know how to do these things until a few years ago.) I also know lots of college kids who don't even know how to make scrambled eggs! They've relied on frozen meals, packaged food, and their moms instead of learning how to do it themselves. For most Millennials, building a piece of IKEA furniture is the handiest work they've ever done . . . and some are using outsourcing services like TaskRabbit to get out of having to do even that.

Young women today don't have the basic skill set their mothers did. And proper tech etiquette (like how to keep a clean inbox) should be seamlessly incorporated into the rest of homemaking advice.

SAN FRANCISCO CHRONICLE

So, it's clear that we're digitally inclined but somewhat domestically incompetent. Where does that leave us? Brace yourself, friends, because the best of both worlds is coming.

TECHNOLOGY AND HOMEMAKING

For every generation, certain technologies were invented to make homemaking easier. During my grandma's time, it was products like Con-Tact paper (decorative shelves were all the rage), Super Glue, and of course, cake mix.

Originally introduced in the 1930s by P. Duff and Sons, cake mix was patented as an "invention [that] relates to a dehydrated flour for use in making pastry products and to a process of making the same." In the same patent document, Mr. Duff stated that traditional cake making "is not only expensive and inconvenient, but necessitates careful measurements and mixing and, therefore, the provision of suitable apparatus therefore. In addition to the above, unsatisfactory results or failure occur too frequently which represent a serious loss of time, of money, of materials and of energy."

How much time and money were being wasted on failed cakes? Research at this time by Betty Crocker and General Mills indicated that American homemakers were baking nearly 1 billion cakes per year.

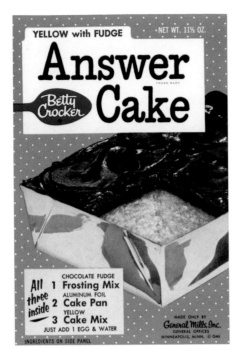

One of the most prominent cake mix brands was Betty Crocker, whose ginger cake mix hit the shelves in 1947. Homemakers welcomed the concept. A traditional recipe for ginger cake had a long list of ingredients, took 13 separate steps, and involved a lot of meticulous measuring and mixing. Even then, the result was sometimes disappointing. But with the Betty Crocker ginger cake mix, all you had to do was add one cup of water and do a little mixing. The cake mix was an instant hit. It came in a relatively small box (14 ounces), so the recipe called for a 9×9-inch pan. Later on, Betty Crocker went so far as to actually give the consumer both the pan and the frosting in addition to the just-add-water mix.

In my mother's age, the microwave, coffeemaker, dishwasher, ice-maker, and sewing machine dramatically reduced the amount of time required to complete household tasks. As my mother's daughter, I can tell you that we used the microwave a lot. Frozen dinners were always in stock at my house. It was the epitome of convenience food.

By 1986, roughly 25% of households in the United States owned a microwave oven, up from only about 1% in 1971. The US Bureau of Labor Statistics reported that over 90% of American households owned a microwave oven in 1997.

Today, in my homemaking era, technology has drastically changed how we operate in our daily lives. We all carry smartphones, own computers, and spend more time online than we do with our families. In fact, the average 18-year-old now spends about six and a half hours online each day. For virtually everything we've ever had to do in the offline world, there's now "an app for that." Take a look at this vintage Radio Shack advertisement from 1991. Every piece of hardware shown now has an app that can replicate its functionality.

Who needs an AM/FM clock radio when we've all got alarm clocks on our phones? Same with calculators, camcorders, scanners, answering machines, speed-dial, and more. And thanks to streaming music services, the fact that people had to spend $159.95 on a CD player that could only play 80 minutes of music is now a laughable concept.

Technology can be expensive, but it can also save you money. For instance, it would have cost $3,054.82 in 1991 to buy all the stuff in the Radio Shack ad. (That's more than $5,000 today adjusted for inflation.) Now you'd be out a couple hundred bucks. Not too shabby.

Technology has also simplified our lives, enabling us to do less of what we may dread, like cooking and cleaning. Now there are gadgets that can clean your floors and windows, and you can use all kinds of apps to order dinner from your phone in under a minute.

Our generation is redefining what it means to be a homemaker. We are connected, employed, and tech-savvy adults who want to have creatively fulfilled lives both in and out of the home. Unlike our parents (and more like our grandparents), we are veering away from big-box brands in favor of those that are local and started by people we may know. We care about being eco-friendly, giving back, and getting social cred for the good things we do. And though we're always interested in saving time whenever we can, we also equally appreciate those who spend hours on end creating something from scratch.

Making is an inherently human activity. We were born to build and create. Think about your life as a child. If you're like most people, someone probably put LEGOs or blocks in front of you. Did you sit there for hours and wonder what to make? No. You just started building! When you were done, you probably surveyed your design and proudly shared it with someone else. Creating something is an act of human expression, and creativity makes us feel alive. Our ancestors could not have survived if they had not been able to make and build, yet these days we take that ability for granted, since we can outsource virtually all creative tasks.

The ability to make things is literally built into our DNA, yet many people haven't let out that side of themselves since they were children. Now, however, our generation seems to be having a creative resurgence. You can see the spillover effect in terms of the food and products we purchase. Before we buy anything, we want to know how it was made, where it comes from, and who made it. This viewpoint is very different from the attitude of the past two or three generations, who just wanted a quick fix or a cheap buy. It's almost as if we're reverting back to the attitudes of our grandparents' and great grandparents' generations during the days where we lacked advertising coming from popular media like television, radio, and the Internet and, instead, solely relied on learning about new brands and products from the local people and places we developed real relationships with.

Here's more proof of the changing times: big brands are now listening to us, understanding our shifting attitudes, and trying to win us over. Throughout the past year, huge companies like Domino's and Starbucks have launched advertising campaigns with messaging about their local and "handcrafted" food and drinks. In one ad, a Domino's employee goes so far as to call his hands his "tools" for crafting pizza. "Made by hand" is a phrase with a whole new meaning for our generation, yet that definition is changing quickly too.

81% of Gen-Xers and Gen-Yers say that if price and quality were equal, they'd prefer to buy a product from another person rather than from a company or a brand.

THE MAKER MOVEMENT

If something is handmade, does that mean it can be hand-designed on a computer screen, translated into a digital file, and then brought to life as a physical object? For many people, the answer is now yes.

Computer-aided design (also referred to as CAD) is a fancy phrase for this type of process and is most often used to describe the design of three-dimensional (3D) objects. Yet there is now an array of software applications that let you virtually design physical objects for production in the real world. These days you can design everything from wallpaper to shoes online, then have your designs fabricated as real-life objects.

While many websites will outsource the actual manufacturing of your designs for you (take custom Nike ID shoes, for example), it is also now possible to use increasingly affordable tools like laser cutters, 3D printers, and CNC (computer numerical control) machines to produce them yourself. And many people are. Millions are now using these machines to create everything from jewelry to electronics, both for themselves and to sell online. This process is now being referred to as "self-manufacturing," a kind of production that takes a lot of the effort and cost out of physically making something new, yet still allows individuals to be designers—or as I prefer to call them, makers.

In my opinion, all of us are makers. If you can operate a computer, you can make things using these modern technologies. This type of innovation has spurred a movement that, since 2008, has been referred to as the "Maker Movement." Some are even calling it "the next Industrial Revolution." This is the first time in history that we have been able to decentralize the manufacturing process. Instead of finding a manufacturer to make a product for me, I can hop onto my computer, download a file, press Print, and have a real-life object pop out of a machine . . . all from the comfort of my home. (Seems like *The Jetsons,* I know.) The barriers have dropped for anyone who has a great invention or idea.

What's more, you don't have to purchase thousands of units just to get a decent price for your product. In fact, you can make just one product for a buck or two using these tools. Case in point: a couple of Christmases ago, I opted out of sending traditional holiday cards in favor of 3D printing custom ornaments for my friends and family instead. I added a message, "Happy Holidays 2013—Love, The Morins," and was able to print 100 in a day. Each one cost me about a quarter. Not only were the ornaments a more customized and creative holiday greeting, but I saved tons of money as well.

The most notable and most talked about technology of the Maker Movement is probably 3D printing, but it's still in its infancy. I like to think of a 3D printer as a high-tech glue gun combined with an inkjet printer. You feed in material (usually plastic, though some new printers can now print materials like ceramic, wood, and even food), and the machine heats it up to the point of melting. Just as with an inkjet printer, you can send a digital file to your 3D printer so that it knows what to print. Once the machine is heated and the file is sent, a small nozzle starts building the product on a platform, from left to right, bottom to top. It uses very fine lines to create a smooth surface. Depending on the size of the product, the printing process can take as little as a few minutes or as long as a few hours. As the technology improves, the speed of printing will vastly increase.

I've used my 3D printer to make all kinds of objects, from home decor pieces like napkin rings and vases to fashion accessories like jewelry. I have many friends with young children who use it to create dollhouse furniture and action figures.

Brands ranging from Gap to Kate Spade better pay attention, because fashion designers and retailers will soon be highly impacted by 3D technology. With new body scanning software, you can do a 360-degree scan of your body and export your precise measurements so that clothing manufacturers can make garments that fit you perfectly. Retailers like Bloomingdale's have already started experimenting with this technology, letting customers do an in-store body scan to find a perfect-fitting pair of jeans. Maybe you have large calves and no boots ever fit you well. Get excited, because soon all your shoes will fit like a glove.

Other major retailers are hopping on this innovation wagon: Victoria's Secret, for instance, is trying to use this technology to help women create their own perfect-fitting bra (hooray!).

My favorite 3D fashion innovation is still years away, but is already proving itself a viable concept: 3D-printed clothing. Yes, soon a machine in your closet will physically weave and stitch together fabric based on a pattern you tell it to print. This means that in a few years you may be able to download an outfit to wear, "print" it out in your closet the same day, and have it fit you perfectly. The best part? Once you're done wearing the outfit, you'll be able to feed it back into the printer to recycle the fibers and reprint something totally new for the next day. Not only will this type of technology make the world more eco-friendly, but it will also help consumers save a few bucks as well. All moms and dads with growing children can rejoice that they won't have to throw away or donate clothes every year. Instead, they can just turn them into something new. I'm especially excited for how this could help the developing world and those in severe poverty.

Will we all have to know how to 3D-design objects to make these things? Nope. In fact, this is the beauty of the Maker Movement. Opensourcing—making your ideas free for others to use, replicate, or modify—is one of the principles driving this movement forward at lightning speed. You can hop online to a website like thingiverse.com and select something to 3D-print from thousands of free designs. From there, you can download the file, modify it if you choose (for example, I modified my Christmas ornament design by adding text on top), and then print it. Now, of course, there are also designs that you must purchase for download, since many designers *do* want to create a business out of their designs. There will always be some combination of free and paid designs, just like you can download free or paid music. In its simplest form, the Maker Movement really means one thing: the democratization of making.

In 2020, the world will have a range of different futures happening concurrently.

GENEVIEVE BELL, DIRECTOR OF INTERACTION AND
EXPERIENCE RESEARCH, INTEL CORPORATION

Beyond fashion and home decor, 3D printing and personalization will also continue to deeply advance the medical industry. Even today, doctors are able to 3D-print human tissues like cartilage and bones. My dog walker, Joustin, had been walking dogs for years. For some reason, an infection started to build in his lower right leg, along his tibia bone. His doctor told him that the infection had spread and it was likely that he would need to have the leg amputated. Luckily, Joustin got a second opinion from a doctor who was more progressive in his use of technology. The doctor figured that if he could take a 3D scan of Joustin's left tibia, he could reprint a replica to use in replacing his right tibia. A crazy idea, but one that Joustin decided was worth taking a chance on. And it worked! As of today, he has two healthy and working legs and is still walking dogs.

More and more people are making, and the demand for makers is increasingly high: 81% of Gen-Xers and Gen-Yers say that if price and quality were equal, they'd prefer to buy a product from another person rather than from a company or a brand, and 64% say that they'd pay 25% more for a product made by an artisan than for one manufactured by a major brand. According to the 2014 Curve Report, a whopping 50% of Gen X and Gen Y women say that they have made an object rather than bought something similar at a store.

The question is no longer, "Will the Maker Movement change the world?" Rather, "How will it change it next?" and "How do you want to change the world?"

FORBES, DECEMBER 2013

Have I convinced you yet that the Maker Movement is a really big deal? The cost of tools like 3D printers and laser cutters is falling dramatically, and I wouldn't be surprised if everyone reading this book has one in their home in the next three to five years. But it's not just machines that are changing the way we create things—it's also the fact that the objects we create can now easily be connected to the Internet.

Despite the fact that, as of 2013, only 14% of 18- to 49-year-olds report having made a product and sold it online, one-third (32%) believe that they will do so by 2018, and three-quarters (74%) say, "If I had the right resources, I believe I could create products that are better than the ones I typically find in stores."

THE INTERNET OF THINGS

There are now over 7 billion mobile phones in the world. Compare that with the fact that there are only a little over 1 billion PCs and you realize how important mobile technology has become to all of us.

Because most of our phones are "smart"—they can connect to the Internet—we are not only using features like GPS (Global Positioning System) and photo-sharing tools more easily, but creating a great deal more data about ourselves than we could have ever done with PCs.

I take my phone with me virtually everywhere I go, and because my phone has GPS and an accelerometer built inside, I can use an app (like Moves, which was recently acquired by Facebook) that tells me how far I've walked, run, driven, or cycled each day. Without thinking, I am able to track my daily activity and calories burned.

And because my phone can connect to my home Wi-Fi network, I can also turn on lights and appliances, change the thermostat, and play music in my home, right from the palm of my hand. In fact, I can even program my home to know it's me pulling into the garage (and not my husband) so that when I come in the door the lights have been dimmed to my preferences, my favorite playlist is playing through the speakers, and the temperature is 72, my preferred in-home climate. Who says technology can't make you feel like a princess?! I'm also able to turn my car on or off, change its temperature, or lock the doors—all from my phone. Soon my car will be able to drive without me at the wheel. I can't wait to tell my kids about what a "driver's license" once was.

Our dogs are getting "smarter" too. My own pup, Pixel, has a "smart collar," which tells me where he is at all times and how much activity he's gotten each day. When Joustin takes him out for a walk, the collar tells me when they left and when they returned.

Even our plants are getting smarter! I use a special device with my plants that can track the dryness of the soil and send me a tweet or email whenever they need watering. There is now even a gardening tool that will water them for you, right when they need it.

Gone are the days of overcooked meals. Now I can get an alert on my phone as soon as my salmon is perfectly baked. You know, because my oven is able to tell. Naturally.

This is the world we're now living in. Everything around us is becoming "connected," and for the most part, that makes our lives easier and more efficient. We have more time to do the things we actually *want* to do, like spend time with friends and family or get creative. The tech industry refers to this trend as "the Internet of Things," which means exactly that—the Internet has evolved from just being on our computers and phones to being connected to actual objects. The impact on our homes is obvious, but the real excitement lies with the makers. The cost, size, and learning curve involved in implanting circuit boards, Wi-Fi networks, GPS, and Bluetooth technology in physical products has dropped significantly over the past few years. As a result, even those who are electronics amateurs have been able to invent products that could change the world. And all for a fraction of the cost and time it used to take.

So what does all of this mean? Let's put the pieces together.

1. The rules and definition of "homemaker" are rapidly changing. This generation is much unlike the past.

2. Everyone is born creative. It's a human trait.

3. Technology is now letting us express our creativity in a way that requires much less time, skill, and money.

4. While everything around us is becoming connected, we're still yearning for an analog balance to our digital lives.

If all of this is true, we have an exciting future ahead. Regardless of whether you believe it will be as big as the next Industrial Revolution, it will definitely change the way we live out our personal lives inside our homes, from the way we cook and entertain to the way we get dressed. Most notably, our ability to balance the digital and analog will become more important than ever before.

1

KITCHEN

The kitchen is my favorite room in the home. In my house, the kitchen is wide open and connects to both the living and dining room, making it the central hub for guests to hang out when they come over. Our counter-height bar is used far more often than our dining table, making it easier to cook and chat together at once. My grandmother would probably just gawk! Back in her day, most kitchens were closed off from the dining and living rooms, so that the chef could cook alone. Who would want that? This generation believes in cooking as a communal experience, not one that hides behind closed doors.

It's also possible that the kitchen is my favorite room because it is one of the most creative places in the home. In the kitchen, "making" happens almost every day and cooking experiments run wild.

In my early twenties, I was a single woman who lived off nothing but cereal and milk. Seriously, I would sometimes have it for every meal of the day—don't judge me. My appreciation for the kitchen has definitely grown since then, especially once I learned all the basic cooking skills and recipes that many of my friends *still* don't know. That's okay, friends; that's what this book is for. Getting to design and build my own kitchen didn't hurt either. Cooking and entertaining are definitely more fun in a space you love to be in. Take some of the tips from this chapter to heart and watch how much more you start to enjoy your own kitchen and cooking!

THE INCREDIBLE EDIBLE EGG

Eggs are one of the most basic (and most healthy) foods, yet many people make mistakes when preparing them. Feast your eyes on the right ways to make an egg—whatever your choice of cooking style!

HARD-BOILED EGGS

Hard-boiled eggs are great to make ahead for adding to salads and sandwiches or even for having a quick and easy breakfast on the go.

Hack:

Ever wonder if that egg is boiled or not? Here's how to tell without cracking open a gooey mess. Spin the egg on a flat surface and then gently touch the top with your finger. If the egg stops spinning, it's boiled; if it continues spinning, it's not. Gotta love the law of inertia!

STEP 1: Put your eggs in a saucepan with one to two inches of water. I always add half a teaspoon of salt to keep the eggs from cracking.

STEP 2: Turn your burner to high and bring your eggs to a boil. Then remove the pan from the heat and cover it while the eggs sit for 10–12 minutes, depending on the number of eggs you are boiling. I recommend hard-boiling three to four at a time.

STEP 3: Remove the eggs with a slotted spoon and immediately place them in a bowl of ice water for two minutes. Remove the eggs from the ice water, store them in the refrigerator, and eat them within five days.

Did you know that to make your hard-boiled eggs easier to peel you should use eggs that are a few days old? Peeling is also a lot easier if you refrigerate the hard-boiled eggs beforehand.

FRIED EGGS

For perfect sunny-side-up eggs, look no further. This tutorial comes straight from my grandma, who used to make me eggs and toast every morning when she visited. Her eggs were always perfect.

Hack:

Crack your egg into a small saucer first, then slide it into the pan. This makes it easier to avoid cracking your yolk prematurely.

STEP 1: Add a pat of butter to a pan. (I find cast iron pans are best because they spread the most even heat, but nonstick pans work well too.) Set heat to medium and let butter slowly melt.

STEP 2: Add your egg to the middle of the pan.

STEP 3: Add a tablespoon or so of water to your pan, then cover with a lid to let the egg steam. This way the egg is cooking from both above and below.

STEP 4: Let the egg cook for four to five minutes, until the egg white is solid and the edges are slightly brown.

STEP 5: Once cooked, transfer the egg to a serving plate and season with salt and pepper.

SCRAMBLED EGGS

Scrambled was probably the first type of eggs you ever cooked, but have you learned to make them the proper way? Perfect scrambled eggs should be slightly wet, light, and creamy, and not in need of cheese to make them taste good. Here's a crash course in scrambled eggs, complete with all the things people do wrong when cooking them.

STEP 1: First, whisk together your eggs in a bowl and add a dollop of milk or cream (about one tablespoon per egg). Be sure to whisk vigorously, as you want to add air and volume to your eggs. This is what makes them fluffy!

> **NOTE 1:** There is a ton of debate about whether to add milk to scrambled eggs. I find that adding milk or cream makes eggs slightly tastier, but you can definitely make fluffy scrambled eggs without them. Try both ways and decide for yourself.

> **NOTE 2:** Don't slack on the whisking! When you're done, you should not see clear lumps of egg white. Instead, the eggs should have the texture of a consistently smooth, yellowish cream.

STEP 2: Add a tablespoon of butter or nonstick spray to your pan (I use olive oil spray) and turn the heat to medium-low.

STEP 3: Pour your eggs into the pan and make sure they spread to the edges.

STEP 4: Wait for about a minute, then start scrambling! Slowly stir your eggs with a wooden spoon or a spatula. Once you notice small lumps forming, turn your heat down to low. This is important, because you don't want to brown or overcook your eggs. (Though, yes, it's annoying because it takes longer to cook them.)

STEP 5: Continue turning your eggs over until there is no liquid left. Try to keep the curds as large as possible—you don't want curds so small you have to use a spoon to eat your eggs.

STEP 6: Add a pinch of salt and pepper once the eggs are nearly done. It's better to season them at the end so that the salt doesn't affect the cooking process.

How "done" you like your eggs is a matter of personal preference. I like to remove my eggs from the pan when they're still slightly moist, as there is enough heat in them that they'll continue cooking once I transfer them to a plate. Others like their eggs dryer. But be careful going too dry—no one likes overcooked eggs.

POACHED EGGS

Love yourself an Eggs Benedict on Sunday morning? Me too! Forget about waiting to get your fix at brunch—follow the steps below to make your own perfectly poached eggs right in the comfort of your own home.

Tip:

If this process sounds too intense for you, or if you're having a hard time keeping your egg whites from feathering, try a tool like the Poachpod, which will let you hack the poaching process.

STEP 1: Add at least three inches of water to a saucepan and bring water to a mild boil. You don't want your water too hot. Be sure it's not boiling too heavily or your eggs won't wind up perfectly rounded. Meanwhile, crack an egg into a small container, such as a cup, ramekin, or small bowl. Different taste preferences have led to many debates about adding vinegar to your eggs; I add it because I feel that vinegar helps to keep the egg whites together. If you're up for it, add half a cup of vinegar to your bowl before adding your egg.

STEP 2: Now the fun part. Using a spoon or whisk, draw circles in the water until you create a whirlpool-like effect in your saucepan. Carefully drop the egg into the center of your whirlpool. The spinning water keeps the egg tightly together as it cooks.

Use a slotted spoon to keep swirling the water and cradling the egg together for two to four minutes—less time for runnier yolks, more time for harder yolks.

STEP 3: Use your spoon to lift the egg out of the water. Set it on a paper towel to dry before transferring it to your bowl or plate.

STEP 4: Add additional eggs one by one, using the same process.

Most people never learn how to properly and easily frost a cake or cupcake. The method you used as a nine-year-old ("spread until covered") doesn't always turn out so great when you're a grown-up. Here are a few easy ways to perfect your frosting skills so that your next baked treat looks as good as it tastes.

ROUNDED CUPCAKE

The basic cupcake frosting technique is rounded on the edges and flat on top. This is probably the style you've seen in many modern bakeries and cake shops.

SUPPLIES

Large round piping tip

Pastry bag

INSTRUCTIONS

STEP 1: Cut off the tip of a pastry bag and insert the large round tip. Fill the bag with frosting and twist the end to close. Center the frosting tip over the cupcake about one centimeter from the surface. Use one hand to simultaneously pinch the end of the bag to keep it closed and cradle the bag of frosting. Use the other hand to guide the piping tip.

STEP 2: Using the hand holding the end of the pastry bag, gently begin squeezing the frosting into the center of the cupcake without moving the tip, until a fluffy, round cloud of frosting starts to form around the tip.

STEP 3: Continue squeezing without moving the tip, until the frosting reaches the edges of the cupcake. Pull the frosting tip up and you're done.

You can use an offset spatula or knife to smooth any peak that forms as you pull the tip away.

STEP 4: Finish things off by dipping the edges of your cupcake in sprinkles.

SWIRLED CUPCAKE

The swirled cupcake, which seems to have been inspired by the look of frozen yogurt, is a classic.

SUPPLIES

Large star tip

Pastry bag

INSTRUCTIONS

STEP 1: Cut off the tip of a pastry bag and insert the large round tip. Fill the bag with frosting and twist the end to close.

STEP 2: Starting at one edge of the cupcake, gently squeeze the frosting to create a perimeter around the edge.

STEP 3: Without stopping, create a smaller circle on top of the first circle, and then complete a smaller third circle on top of the second until you close the opening.

STEP 4: Use a slight dipping motion to pull the frosting tip away from the top of the cupcake and create a peak.

STEP 5: If you like, top with a smattering of sprinkles.

SWIRLED CAKE

First, I'll take you through the swirled frosting technique. This is an easy way for budding bakers to flex their creative frosting skills. It's tough to mess this one up, so don't be nervous about giving it your all.

SUPPLIES

Large offset spatula

Three 9-inch round pans

Mixing bowls

Mixer

Mixing spoons

INGREDIENTS

2 boxes chocolate cake mix

3 jars vanilla frosting (or any frosting of your choice)

INSTRUCTIONS

STEP 1: Bake cake as instructed, in three separate layers. Let cool. Place one cake layer on a plate.

STEP 2: Spread a thick layer of frosting over the top of the cake layer and top with another cake layer.

STEP 3: Repeat the process with each layer, until you get to your final layer. Do not frost the top yet. Place in the freezer for 20 minutes.

STEP 4: Remove the cake from the freezer and cover the entire cake with the "crumb coat": a thin layer of frosting that seals in the crumbs before you cover the cake with the final layer of frosting. Place the cake in the freezer for another 20 minutes.

STEP 5: Remove the cake from the freezer and cover with a very thick layer of frosting.

STEP 6: Beginning at the top, create small circles on the surface of the frosting using the tip of an offset spatula.

STEP 7: Repeat across the top and sides of the cake until the entire cake has a swirled effect.

NOTES

OMBRE CAKE

Ombre is a design trend that seems to be here to stay, and the cake decorating department is no exception. Follow along to see how to make an ombre layer cake that is also frosted in an ombre style.

SUPPLIES

Large offset spatula

Four 9-inch round pans

Mixing bowls

Mixer

Mixing spoons

INGREDIENTS

2 boxes vanilla cake mix

3 jars vanilla frosting

Food coloring

INSTRUCTIONS

STEP 1: Divide your cake batter into four bowls and add food coloring to tint each bowl of batter. I made bowls of batter that were dark pink (eight to ten drops of red food coloring), medium pink (four to six drops of red), light pink (two to three drops of red), and white (no food coloring).

STEP 2: In another four bowls, divide your frosting in even amounts and mix with food coloring to match each cake layer.

STEP 3: Bake as directed and let cool.

STEP 4: Place the darkest cake layer on a plate. Spread a thick layer of matching frosting over the top of the cake layer and around the sides. Top with the next lighter cake layer and repeat the process with the remaining layers. Place in the freezer for 20 minutes.

STEP 5: Now it's time to create your crumb coat. You'll create a crumb coat that is ombre, just like the final coat of frosting. That's right—you have to ombre your frosting twice!

STEP 6: Remove the cake from the freezer and spread a thick layer of the darkest frosting around the bottom cake layer.

STEP 7: Repeat with the next lighter color of frosting around the next cake layer, and repeat with each color of frosting until you reach the top.

STEP 8: Cover the top layer with a thick layer of the lightest colored frosting.

Pro Tip:

Keep a carafe of hot water on hand. Dip your offset spatula into the water before smoothing the frosting.

STEP 9: Hold the offset spatula parallel to the sides of the cake and smooth the frosting by gently pressing the spatula along the sides of the cake.

STEP 10: Once you have a smooth and thick outer layer of frosting, use the tip of the offset spatula to drag a line around the base of the cake. This works best if you can put the cake on a lazy susan to turn it while you hold the spatula still.

STEP 11: Repeat the process by creating another line directly above the first line, and continue until you reach the top. You can either continue the circular pattern on the top of the cake or leave it smooth.

NOTES

KNIFE SKILLS 101

To be a ninja in the kitchen, you've gotta get down with some serious knife skills. From perfectly minced garlic to well-sliced avocado, here's everything you need to know to get your chop on.

HOW TO MINCE GARLIC

STEP 1: Press your knife flat on a garlic clove to loosen up the skin. This makes it way easier to peel.

STEP 2: Cut the garlic clove into very thin slices.

STEP 3: Turn your knife perpendicular to the slices and begin chopping.

STEP 4: Continue to chop into very fine pieces using an up-and-down motion.

That's it!

HOW TO SLICE AN AVOCADO

STEP 1: Slice the avocado in half by running your knife around the skin of the avocado, using the pit as an anchor.

STEP 2: Use your knife to pull out the pit, then chuck the pit in the trash.

STEP 3: Use a paring knife to cut vertical slits into each half.

STEP 4: Use a spoon to scoop out.

How yummy does that look?

HOW TO CHOP AN ONION

STEP 1: Cut both ends off of the onion, and then cut the onion in half lengthwise. Peel off the papery outer layer.

STEP 2: Place one half of the onion flat side down on the chopping board and slice thinly, almost, but not quite through the end.

STEP 3: Then turn the onion and slice perpendicular to the previous cuts to create chopped pieces.

HOW TO DICE ROUND FRUITS AND VEGGIES

STEP 1: We'll use an eggplant for this one. The first thing to do is cut off the stem.

STEP 2: Then slice the eggplant in half.

STEP 3: Lay the eggplant flat side down and slice lengthwise across while holding it together.

STEP 4: Hold the eggplant together and turn sideways to slice perpendicular to your previous cuts.

COMMON COOKING TERMS

In case you're not very familiar with cooking, here's a quick brushup on some of the most common cooking methods. These are really important to know if you're going to follow recipes correctly, so pay attention!

SAUTÉ
Pan-frying foods such as onions to precook them before they are used in a recipe.

ROAST
Using dry heat to cook food such as fish, meat, poultry, and some fruits and vegetables.

BAKE
Using dry heat to cook foods such as breads, cakes, pies, cookies, and similar foods.

BROIL
Cooking with direct heat from above using the broiler unit in the oven.

BOIL
Heating liquid to the point that bubbles constantly rise to the surface and break.

SIMMER

Heating liquid to the point that bubbles form slowly and break before they reach the surface.

STEAM

Cooking food in steam, usually by placing a steamer basket inside a pan with a small amount of boiling water and covering the pan to keep the steam inside.

FRY

Cooking food in small or large amounts of fat, such as vegetable oil.

BASTE

Brushing or pouring liquid over food, such as a turkey, as it cooks.

No matter whether you're dieting or not, it's always good to know a few tricks for healthier eating. I use the following chart of substitutions all the time while cooking and find the outcomes to be just as delicious. Try it out for your next meal and see for yourself.

1 egg	= 2 egg whites
Sour cream or mayonnaise	= Plain fat-free Greek yogurt
Oil	= Applesauce
Cream cheese	= Pureed cottage cheese
Pasta	= Spaghetti squash
Potatoes	= Mashed cauliflower
Sugar	= Applesauce, agave, honey
Butter	= Applesauce, mashed banana, fat-free Greek yogurt, or avocado

Tips from the Co:

WHAT'S YOUR FAVORITE COOKING HACK?

When in doubt, improvise and substitute. Most herbs and spices can be substituted for another.

Use high-quality olive oil. So worth it!

Food-process Doritos and use them as chicken skin.

When I'm baking chocolate chip cookies, I add a pinch of cinnamon or allspice to give them some more depth of flavor. Another super easy trick that I've learned is to freeze leftovers flat in a Ziploc bag, so they can be arranged like a library in the freezer.

There's always one ingredient (or more) in a recipe that can be purchased in a more convenient form to save cooking time. Lentils? I buy them pre-cooked. Butternut squash? I'll take a pre-cubed bag, please. Garlic? That jar of pre-minced cloves looks pretty appealing. I find that I am able to accomplish a larger variety and more difficult recipes by helping myself along with a few shortcuts.

My favorite cooking hack is to add a bit of brown sugar when making tomato sauce to lower the acidity of the tomatoes and balance it out more. I also add a bit of beer to batter to make it smoother.

Add two teaspoons of vanilla extract and half a teaspoon of lemon extract to boxed cake or cupcake mix to make it taste like you spent hours doing it from scratch.

Add a tablespoon of cream cheese to the center of unrolled Pillsbury crescent rolls. Roll, bake, and as soon as they come out, add confectioners' sugar on top for a wonderful dessert.

Less isn't always more! Experiment with spices!

I always add a spoonful of cocoa powder to dishes that need an earthy kick. Cocoa powder amps up the flavor of chili, stew, and even French onion soup.

Let's face it, sometimes after a whole load of cooking, airing the house is not enough, so I boil a pan of coffee on the stove—works every time (thanks, Mum!).

You won't believe this one but here goes: You know how when you go to the bakery and you see those gorgeous cakes and you think, "How is it possible that the icing looks like that?" You can get that smooth near-fondant look by investing about $3 into your cake. Take one small bag of confectioners' sugar and add to a mixer. Next, find your favorite flavored icing (I love cream cheese!) and throw that in there too. Turn on the mixer. Apply with a flat spatula. Voilà! (You're welcome!) Bonus: It accepts dyes well and the confectioners' sugar doesn't change the taste of the icing—so it doesn't taste overly sugary.

Use a double-folded paper towel to store leafy greens. You will be amazed at the extended time they'll last before they go brown and smelly.

To cook perfect hard-boiled eggs, I poke a tiny hole in the larger end and put them in boiling water for ten minutes, followed by an ice bath. The shells come off easily every time!

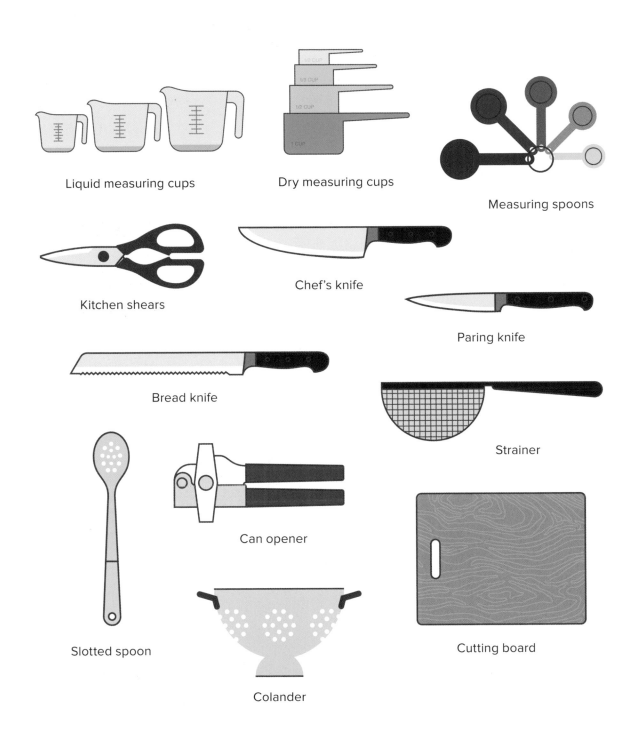

Liquid measuring cups

Dry measuring cups

Measuring spoons

Kitchen shears

Chef's knife

Paring knife

Bread knife

Strainer

Slotted spoon

Can opener

Cutting board

Colander

Skillet

Saucepan/pot

Casserole dish

Baking sheet

Cooling rack

Rubber scraper

Mixing bowls

Cupcake/muffin pan

Mixing spoon

Tongs

Spatulas

APPS

I have so many cooking apps on my phone that I had to make a folder to contain them! And while I still use an occasional cookbook, I get most of my recipe inspiration and instruction from some of the following favorites.

ZIPLIST: Great for extracting a grocery list out of recipes you want to make.

FOODILY: A social network of food! There are millions of recipes for you to browse and search through, with comments from those who have made them.

FOODPAIRING: If you're more of a scientist or pro chef, you will appreciate this app, which lets you mix and match ingredients and aromas to develop entirely new dishes  that have been scientifically proven to excite your taste buds.

EVERNOTE FOOD: Was that meal one to remember? Then make sure you do! Evernote Food is my go-to app for recording all of the delicious things I eat so that I can make sure to eat them over and over again.

PANNA: This app is both a digital magazine and a step-by-step cooking utility. Made for iPad, it features hundreds of video recipes so that you can cook alongside a pro chef, just like in a private cooking class.

GADGETS

SODASTREAM: This one has been around for a while, but it has to be first on the list, since I owe it everything for helping me drink more water. If still water isn't your thing, just dip your cup under the SodaStream and watch it turn fizzy. The flavor add-ons are fun to try too!

VITAMIX: Yes, I qualify my Vitamix as a gadget. This thing is a *beast*. Put any food in it, and it will instantly be turned from solid to liquid. The best part? Cleanup is a snap. Pro chefs and home cooks alike will agree that this investment changes the way you cook. PS: Turn to page 385 to see my daily green juice smoothie recipe made with this blender.

SODASTREAM

SMART CROCKPOT: The crockpot is the one device it's okay to leave on while you are away from home, which is especially necessary given some of the prolonged cooking times of crockpot recipes. (Some take more than five hours!) Now that there's a smart crockpot, you no longer have to worry about whether your food is too rare or overdone—you can control the entire thing from your phone, including cooking time and temperature, no matter where you are.

EGGMINDER: With this device, you'll never again ask: "Do we have any eggs left?" It works by detecting how many eggs are left in the tray, alerting you by phone if the inventory gets too low. As a bonus, it also alerts you if your eggs are going bad.

RANGE OR iGRILL: I'm the worst at guesstimating how well done my meat is. Enter the iGrill. Stick this thermometer in your chicken or beef while it cooks and as soon as the meat is cooked to perfection you'll be alerted by phone. Yum.

BREVILLE SMART SCOOP ICE CREAM MAKER:

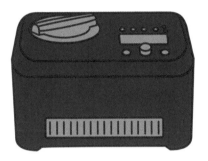

Gone are the days of taking 12 hours or more to prepare a batch of homemade ice cream. I personally love this gadget for its ability to whip up a pint or two in under an hour. Not only that, but you can program it to make sorbet, gelato, yogurt, or ice cream . . . plus mix in all the yummy toppings you want. Try our recipe for basic homemade vanilla ice cream (page 111), then experiment with your own mixtures.

VERTICAL RABBIT WINE OPENER: Okay, so it's not really a "gadget," but it is pretty high-tech. Thirty-one different parts make up this corkscrew, which can pop a bottle of wine in under three seconds. Don't lie, you know that's impressive. Plus, you'll never have to fidget with a manual corkscrew in front of your friends again. #winning

PREP PAD: Take a deep breath, because this one is kind of magical. Made by a company called Orange Chef, the Prep Pad can detect most types of food you place on it, including their weight and their nutritional status. It will display all of this information back to you via an accompanying iPad app.

CHEFSLEEVE: If you cook with an iPad and always have dirty fingers (it's okay, I taste-test with my fingers too!), then this gizmo is for you. Just slip it over your tablet and cook on!

SERVICES

RECIPE DELIVERY:

Companies like Blue Apron and Plated are popping up and serving all parts of the nation by delivering all of the ingredients for a complete  meal. This means you get to skip out on grocery shopping, yet still enjoy all the fun of cooking! I especially like how innovative Blue Apron's recipes are. Try it once for dinner with a few friends and they will surely think you're a cooking pro.

GROCERY DELIVERY:

Everyone from Amazon to Google is vying to win the virtual grocery shopping market that has emerged over the past couple of years. With this new type of service, you log on and shop from all of your local grocery stores. After you check out, your food is delivered  directly to your home in a matter of hours, sometimes sooner. I use these services every week for the staple foods I need, but still hit the stores when I want to spend more time picking out fruits and veggies or discovering new foods.

NOTES

Tips from the Co:

WHICH HOME GADGET COULD YOU NOT LIVE WITHOUT?

The most important gadgets, in order of the most answers received:

Blender

Tablet/computer

Smartphone

KitchenAid mixer (read on, these folks are seriously devoted)

I cannot live without my KitchenAid mixer. I even traveled to my mother's house with it when I was asked to make desserts for our family gathering.

My KitchenAid mixer! Seriously, I don't know how I lived without one or why anyone would choose not to have it on his or her countertop. Want fluffy pancakes? Mixer! Dense, savory meat loaf? Mixer! Ever tried to stand there tearing chicken into shredded bits for a taco recipe? Me neither because I use my mixer for that too!

Other gadgets mentioned:

Coffeemaker

DVR/Netflix/Apple TV

Wine stopper

BREAKFAST

I really do believe that breakfast is the most important meal of the day. I've already taken you through the wonders of the incredible, edible egg—now it's time to delve into my favorite weekend brunch.

SEEDED BAGELS

Makes 12 bagels / Serves 8–16

What's better than a freshly baked bagel? Answer: a homemade freshly baked bagel covered with healthy seeds! This basic bagel recipe takes it to the next level thanks to pumpkin seeds, sunflower seeds, and chia seeds. Yum!

INGREDIENTS

1 packet active dry yeast

1½ cups warm water (110°F–120°F)

4 cups bread flour

1 tablespoon salt

2 tablespoons sugar

1 large egg white

1 tablespoon water

½ cup pumpkin seeds

¼ cup sunflower seeds, salted

¼ cup chia seeds

INSTRUCTIONS

STEP 1: In a stand mixer fitted with the bread hook attachment, dissolve yeast in water and let sit five minutes, or until foamy.

STEP 2: In a separate bowl, combine the flour, salt, and sugar. Add the flour mixture to the water mixture and mix on low with an electric mixer until most of the flour has been incorporated and the dough starts to come together.

STEP 3: Increase speed to medium and continue to mix until dough becomes smooth and elastic, about four minutes, adding small additional amounts of flour if dough is too sticky.

STEP 4: Transfer dough to medium bowl that has been lightly oiled, and let sit for 30 minutes. (Dough will not double in size.) Meanwhile, bring a large pot of water to boil and preheat oven to 400°F.

STEP 5: Lay the dough on a piece of parchment or wax paper. Divide the dough into 12 equal portions and shape each portion into a ball. Gently poke a hole in the center of each ball and stretch slightly to create a larger opening. Let rest for 10 minutes.

STEP 6: Place a few bagels at a time in the boiling water, stretching slightly to increase the opening in the middle. Boil for 30 seconds on each side and remove to a drying rack.

STEP 7: Mix together the egg white and water and brush onto the top of each bagel. Top with seeds.

STEP 8: Place bagels on a baking sheet and bake for 20 to 25 minutes, or until bagels have developed a golden brown color. Let sit at least 15 minutes before serving.

EGG CUPS

Makes 4 egg cups / Serves 4

These egg cups are my favorite brunch party trick. Because each is baked in its own ramekin, you can make as many or as few as you like. You can even let guests or family members customize them by providing a bar of different mix-ins and toppings.

INGREDIENTS

2 cups frozen spinach, thawed and squeezed of excess water

¼ cup Parmesan cheese, shredded

8 slices prosciutto

4 eggs

Salt and pepper to taste

INSTRUCTIONS

STEP 1: Preheat oven to 350°F. Mix together the spinach and Parmesan cheese.

STEP 2: Line four ramekins with prosciutto. Scoop one-quarter of the spinach and cheese mixture into each ramekin and top with an egg.

STEP 3: Place ramekins on a baking sheet and bake for 20 to 30 minutes, depending on desired degree of doneness.

LUNCH

Now on to lunch! For this midday meal, I'll show you how to make three classic comfort foods that everyone should know how to prepare: Caesar salad, tomato soup, and grilled cheese.

TOMATO SOUP

Serves 4

There's no better comfort food on a cool day than tomato soup. And even on a warm day, it can be chilled for a tasty treat. You could buy your soup in a can, of course, but it's always good to know at least one handmade soup recipe to impress your family and friends. This is by far one of the easiest to master.

INGREDIENTS

1 tablespoon butter

¼ cup onions, chopped

¼ cup celery, chopped

¼ cup carrots, chopped

1 clove garlic, minced

1 28-ounce can San Marzano tomatoes

4 cups vegetable or chicken broth

½ cup half-and-half

2 tablespoons basil, chopped

INSTRUCTIONS

STEP 1: Over medium-low heat, sauté the onion in butter in a large stockpot until the onions have softened, about five minutes.

STEP 2: Add the celery, carrots, and garlic and cook for another five minutes.

STEP 3: Add the tomatoes and broth to the stockpot and bring the soup to a boil. Reduce heat and let simmer for 30 minutes.

STEP 4: Remove the pot from the heat and pour in the half-and-half. Using an immersion blender or stand-up blender, puree the soup until smooth. Ladle the soup into bowls and garnish with the fresh basil.

CAESAR SALAD

Serves 4

Who doesn't love Caesar Salad? The great thing about this recipe is that you can make substitutes for the mayo (try using low-fat mayo or even Greek yogurt) to keep calorie portions in check. It's an easy go-to dish that will take minutes to perfect.

INGREDIENTS FOR THE CAESAR DRESSING

2 cloves garlic, minced

½ teaspoon anchovy paste (optional)

2 tablespoons lemon juice

1 teaspoon Dijon mustard

1 tablespoon red wine vinegar

1 dash Worcestershire sauce

2 tablespoons mayonnaise

½ cup olive oil

Salt and pepper to taste

INGREDIENTS FOR THE CROUTONS

2 tablespoons butter

¼ loaf bread, cut into 1-inch cubes

INGREDIENTS FOR THE SALAD

Romaine lettuce

Caesar dressing

Croutons

Parmesan cheese, grated

INSTRUCTIONS FOR THE CAESAR DRESSING

In a glass measuring cup or blender, mix together all of the ingredients except the olive oil and salt and pepper. Slowly drizzle in the olive oil while whisking constantly, until the dressing is uniform in texture. Season with the salt and pepper to taste.

INSTRUCTIONS FOR THE CROUTONS

Melt the butter in a large sauté pan over medium heat. Add the bread cubes and cook for five minutes, or until they begin to brown on most sides. Set aside and let cool.

INSTRUCTIONS FOR THE SALAD

Chop the romaine lettuce horizontally into one-inch strips and place in a large salad bowl. Toss with the dressing and top with croutons and Parmesan cheese.

ADULT GRILLED CHEESE

Makes 4 sandwiches

By far my favorite comfort food of all time, the grilled cheese sandwich not only brings back memories of childhood but also happens to pair well with tomato soup! Gone are the days when you put processed sliced cheese inside a couple of pieces of bread. This recipe is a definite upgrade from the lunchtime classic you enjoyed as a ten-year-old. Play with different types of cheeses and breads until you find your perfect combo.

INGREDIENTS

¼ cup apricot jam

1 loaf French or sourdough bread, thickly sliced

8 slices prosciutto

4 ounces Gruyère cheese, grated

2 tablespoons butter

INSTRUCTIONS

STEP 1: Spread one tablespoon of the jam over one side of a slice of bread. Top with two slices of prosciutto and 2¼ teaspoons grated Gruyère cheese. Top with another slice of bread.

STEP 2: Heat a medium sauté pan over medium-low heat and add ½ tablespoon of butter. Place the sandwich in the pan and heat on each side until golden brown and the cheese is melted, about five minutes per side.

STEP 3: Repeat with the remaining three sandwiches. Cut each sandwich in half before serving.

DINNER

Dinner is your time to shine as a cook. It's the most common meal to share with family and friends, so you'll want to have at least one go-to dish that you can prep in under an hour or two. Make sure you always have a main and a couple of sides (ideally at least one veggie dish) to add a variety of taste and nutrition to the table.

ROASTED CHICKEN

Serves 4

Most people get crazy intimidated by the idea of cooking a whole chicken (or a turkey on Thanksgiving), but fear not! I swear it's way easier than you think.

INGREDIENTS

2 tablespoons rosemary, chopped

2 cloves garlic, chopped

1 tablespoon lemon zest

1 tablespoon sea salt

1 tablespoon pepper

1 whole chicken, 4–5 pounds

INSTRUCTIONS

STEP 1: Preheat oven to 400°F.

STEP 2: Create a paste by chopping all of the ingredients except for the whole chicken together.

STEP 3: Rub the mixture all over the chicken and under the skin, if desired. Bake for about 15 minutes per pound, or one hour for a four-pound bird. Use a meat thermometer placed in the thickest part of the thigh and breast to check for doneness (about 165°F). Let sit 15 minutes before serving.

Tips:

Salt vs. Acid

1. Salt makes food taste flavorful instead of flat. Hardly any dish is complete without salt, even desserts. Add salt slowly to dishes to avoid overseasoning. Only add to sauces after they've been reduced.

2. Acids make your mouth water. Wondering why that sauce still doesn't taste right after salting? Squeeze some citrus or vinegar in there to give it a lift. And if you make something too sour, add fat or sugar to combat the pucker.

THREE WAYS TO USE LEFTOVER ROAST CHICKEN

Whether you're cooking for one, two, or three, you may end up with quite a few leftovers in the roast chicken department. Lucky for you, roast chicken is so versatile that it's a great thing to keep on hand. Here are three of my favorite ways to use those yummy leftovers.

CHICKEN SALAD SANDWICH

Makes 2 sandwiches

I love adding a bit of sweetness and crunch to the standard chicken salad. In this recipe, red grapes are the sweet and the pecans add a punch of extra crunch.

INGREDIENTS

2 cups roasted chicken, chopped

¼ cup celery, chopped

½ cup red grapes, halved and chopped

½ cup pecans, chopped

¼ to ½ cup low-fat mayonnaise

4 slices thick-cut bread

INSTRUCTIONS

In a large bowl, mix together all the ingredients except the bread. Lightly toast the bread and top two slices with a healthy helping of chicken salad. Top each with another slice of bread and cut in half before serving.

CHICKEN NOODLE SOUP

Serves 2

The classic chicken noodle soup gets an upgrade in this roast chicken remix.

INGREDIENTS

1 tablespoon butter

½ cup onions, chopped

½ cup celery, chopped

½ cup carrots, roughly chopped

2 cups roasted chicken, shredded

4 cups chicken broth

2 cups egg noodles

Salt and pepper to taste

Juice from 1 lemon

Chopped parsley for garnish

INSTRUCTIONS

STEP 1: In a large stockpot, heat the butter over medium heat until melted.

STEP 2: Add the onions, celery, and carrots, cooking until the vegetables begin to soften.

STEP 3: Add the chicken and chicken broth, bring to a boil, and then reduce to a simmer for 15 minutes.

STEP 4: Add the noodles and cook for another 10 minutes, or according to package directions.

STEP 5: Add the salt, pepper, and lemon juice to taste.

STEP 6: Garnish with the fresh chopped parsley.

CHICKEN TACOS

Makes 4 tacos / Serves 2

This healthier taco alternative subs in goat cheese for sour cream and cheddar cheese, cabbage leaves for tortillas, and corn and black bean salsa for taco sauce.

INGREDIENTS

1 red cabbage

2 cups chicken, shredded

1 mango, diced

¼ cup goat cheese, crumbled

¼ cup corn and black bean salsa

Cilantro for garnish

INSTRUCTIONS

Peel four leaves from the red cabbage. Top each with ½ cup of chicken, a tablespoon or two of chopped mango, a sprinkle of goat cheese, and a dollop of salsa. Top with a few sprigs of cilantro for garnish.

MAC 'N' CHEESE

Serves 4

Really, is there anything better than a good bowl of mac 'n' cheese? If you've never made it yourself (it's okay, I too confess to occasionally eating the packaged variety), you're missing out on a flavor explosion in your mouth. Try this recipe as a side dish for any meal, and once you master it, wow your friends by bringing it to your next potluck dinner party.

INGREDIENTS

16 ounces elbow pasta

2 tablespoons butter

2 tablespoons flour

2 cups milk (2% or higher)

½ cup sharp cheddar cheese, shredded

½ cup Asiago cheese, shredded

½ cup Gruyère cheese, shredded

½ cup mozzarella cheese, shredded

Salt and pepper to taste

INSTRUCTIONS

STEP 1: Fill a large pot with water and bring to a boil. Add the pasta and cook according to package directions. Drain and set aside.

STEP 2: Meanwhile, melt the butter in a large saucepan. Add the flour and let the mixture begin to bubble, stirring constantly for one minute to cook the flour.

STEP 3: Slowly add the milk to the mixture and continue to cook over medium-low heat until the mixture is thickened and creamy, stirring constantly.

STEP 4: Add all the cheeses and stir until melted and creamy. Add the pasta and toss to combine. Season to taste and serve immediately.

ROASTED VEGETABLES

All vegetables should be roasted at a relatively high heat of 450°F to ensure browning. The timing suggestions here will help you avoid overcooking your veggies. Toss the vegetables with some olive oil, salt, pepper, and other seasonings of your choice before popping them into the oven.

Vegetable	Prep	Time
Asparagus	Whole	10–15 minutes
Broccoli	1- to 2-inch pieces	15–20 minutes
Cauliflower	1- to 2-inch pieces	20–25 minutes
Brussels sprouts	Halved	30–35 minutes
Potatoes	2-inch pieces	40–45 minutes
Turnips	1½-inch pieces	40–45 minutes
Onions	2-inch pieces	15–20 minutes
Carrots	1-inch pieces	30–35 minutes
Butternut squash	1-inch pieces	25–30 minutes
Sweet potatoes	2-inch pieces	30–35 minutes

BANANA SPLIT CAKE

Serves 12

Are you ready for a dessert that's an epic combination of flavors and colors? Why not combine the flavors of a banana split with the craft of a perfectly layered cake? Cherries, chocolate sauce, and whipped cream are all involved. My favorite part is obviously the banana buttercream frosting. Nom.

This style of cake is called a "naked cake," meaning you won't be frosting the outer edge of the cake. This technique is popular with colorful cakes like this one, and don't worry—there's plenty of buttercream frosting in between each cake layer to make up for a lack of frosting on the outside.

INGREDIENTS FOR THE STRAWBERRY CAKE LAYER

1 cup butter, softened

1⅔ cups sugar

1 3-ounce package strawberry gelatin (such as Jell-O®)

4 large egg whites

2¾ cups cake flour

1 tablespoon baking powder

1 teaspoon salt

1 cup whole milk

2 teaspoons vanilla

INGREDIENTS FOR THE VANILLA CAKE LAYER

1 cup butter, softened

2 cups sugar

4 large egg whites

2¾ cups cake flour

1 tablespoon baking powder

1 teaspoon salt

1 cup whole milk

2 teaspoons vanilla

INGREDIENTS FOR THE CHOCOLATE CAKE LAYER

2 cups sugar

2 cups all-purpose flour

¾ cup unsweetened cocoa powder

1½ teaspoons baking powder

1½ teaspoons baking soda

1 teaspoon salt

2 eggs

1 cup buttermilk

½ cup butter, melted

2 teaspoons vanilla

1 cup hot coffee or water

INGREDIENTS FOR THE BANANA BUTTERCREAM FROSTING

1 cup butter, softened

3 ripe bananas

1 tablespoon vanilla

1 pound confectioners' sugar

1 cup buttermilk

INGREDIENTS FOR THE TOPPINGS

Canned whipped cream

Maraschino cherries

Chocolate sauce

Sprinkles

INSTRUCTIONS FOR THE STRAWBERRY CAKE

STEP 1: Preheat oven to 350°F. Grease and flour one 9-inch cake pan.

STEP 2: In a large bowl or stand mixer, beat the butter on medium-high speed until it is light and fluffy. Add the sugar and strawberry gelatin and beat until incorporated. Reduce mixer speed to medium and add the egg whites one at a time, beating after each addition.

STEP 3: In a separate bowl, mix together the flour, baking powder, and salt. Also separately, mix together the milk and vanilla in a liquid measuring cup.

STEP 4: Add one-third of the flour mixture to the butter, mixing until just combined. Follow with half of the milk mixture, mixing again until just combined. Repeat the process until all ingredients are fully combined.

STEP 5: Pour the mixture into the cake pan and place in the oven. Bake for 25 to 35 minutes, or until a toothpick inserted in the middle of the cake comes out clean.

STEP 6: Remove the cake from the oven and let cool for five minutes. Then run a knife around the edge and turn the pan over to remove the cake. Let cool completely before frosting.

INSTRUCTIONS FOR THE VANILLA CAKE

STEP 1: Preheat oven to 350°F. Grease and flour one 9-inch cake pan.

STEP 2: In a large bowl or stand mixer, beat the butter on medium-high speed until it is light and fluffy. Add the sugar and beat until incorporated. Reduce the mixer speed to medium and add the egg whites one at a time, beating after each addition.

STEP 3: In a separate bowl, mix together the flour, baking powder, and salt. Also separately, mix together the milk and vanilla in a liquid measuring cup.

STEP 4: Add one-third of the flour mixture to the butter, mixing until just combined. Follow with half of the milk mixture, mixing again until just combined. Repeat the process until all ingredients are fully combined.

STEP 5: Pour the mixture into the cake pan and place in the oven. Bake for 25 to 35 minutes, or until a toothpick inserted in the middle of the cake comes out clean.

STEP 6: Remove the cake from the oven and let cool for five minutes. Then run a knife around the edge and turn the pan over to remove the cake. Let cool completely before frosting.

INSTRUCTIONS FOR THE CHOCOLATE CAKE

STEP 1: Preheat oven to 350°F. Grease and flour one 9-inch cake pan.

STEP 2: In a large bowl or stand mixer, stir together the sugar, flour, cocoa powder, baking powder, baking soda, and salt. Add all of the wet ingredients and mix on medium speed for about two minutes.

STEP 3: Pour the mixture into the cake pan and place in the oven. Bake for 25 to 35 minutes, or until a toothpick inserted in the middle of the cake comes out clean.

STEP 4: Remove the cake from the oven and let cool for five minutes. Then run a knife around the edge and turn the pan over to remove the cake. Let cool completely before frosting.

INSTRUCTIONS FOR THE BANANA BUTTERCREAM FROSTING

In a large bowl or stand mixer, beat the butter on medium-high speed for three minutes or until fluffy. Add the bananas, vanilla, half of the confectioners' sugar, and half the milk. Mix in gradually on low speed until incorporated, and then add remaining confectioners' sugar and milk. Beat on low speed again until just mixed, and then increase speed to medium-high until the frosting is uniform in texture and fluffy.

INSTRUCTIONS FOR ASSEMBLY

STEP 1: Place one cake layer on a plate. Fill a pastry bag fitted with a large round tip with frosting. Outline the top edge of the cake layer with frosting, and then fill in the center with frosting until the top of the cake layer is covered in a thick, uniform layer of frosting. Place the cake in the freezer for 20 minutes.

STEP 2: Remove the cake from the freezer and repeat with the next two layers, freezing the cake for 20 minutes each time before adding the next layer.

STEP 3: Just before you are ready to serve the cake, use a can of whipped cream to pipe dollops of cream around the top edge of the cake. Top each dollop with a Maraschino cherry and drizzle with chocolate sauce. Finish off with sprinkles and you're done!

Tips:
Cake Hacks
1. Wrap and tie a thick piece of fabric (like a rolled-up T-shirt) around your cake pan before placing it in the oven to help create flatter cakes that are easier to layer.

2. Use a lazy susan to frost a cake more easily. Just spin as you frost!

3. No knife? No problem. Try using dental floss to cut your cake. It's strong enough and will create a smooth cut.

NOTES

HOMEMADE VANILLA ICE CREAM

Makes about 1 quart / Serves 8

Making your own creamy vanilla ice cream is not quite as easy as buying store-bought, but making your own can be a *lot* easier if you've got an ice cream maker! This recipe serves as a great base for lots of different flavor combinations. My favorite mix-ins are strawberries, sprinkles, and a few pieces of shaved chocolate.

INGREDIENTS

1 cup whole milk

¾ cup granulated sugar

¼ teaspoon salt

1 vanilla bean

2 cups heavy cream

6 large egg yolks

1 teaspoon vanilla

OPTIONAL TOPPINGS

Sprinkles

Chocolate chips

Strawberries

TOOLS

Ice cream maker

INSTRUCTIONS

STEP 1: Add the milk, sugar, and salt to a medium saucepan. Split the vanilla bean in half and scrape the seeds into the mixture, followed by the pod.

STEP 2: Bring the mixture to a simmer over medium-low heat and then remove from heat. Cover and set aside for one hour to let the vanilla bean steep.

STEP 3: Reheat the mixture over medium-low heat. Meanwhile, stir together the cream and eggs in another bowl until fully incorporated.

STEP 4: Gradually add the warmed milk mixture to the eggs, stirring constantly to keep the eggs from cooking (this is called "tempering" the eggs). Return the entire mixture back to the saucepan and heat until thick enough to coat the back of a wooden spoon, for about five minutes. Place the ice cream mixture in the refrigerator until completely cool. Process in an ice cream maker according to the manufacturer's directions.

NOTES

THE FUTURE KITCHEN

If you thought today's modern kitchen appliances were cool, you have no idea what's coming next. The future kitchen will smartly keep an inventory of all the food inside it and suggest recipes based on that inventory; in fact, kitchens a few years from now will even do most of the cooking for you. Of course, those who still want to do the cooking themselves will be able to turn their stove or oven to "manual" and make a meal the old-fashioned way. Regardless of how technology will help you cook, I'm just excited that we'll all be making more creative and delicious meals at home in much less time.

SMART KNIFE: Though it is still just a concept, this knife could soon become a reality. It's basically a chef's knife doubling as a tablet that can detect and display—right on its blade—information about what it's cutting, including freshness level and nutritional information. How 'bout them apples? (Get it?)

NANO GARDEN: If you haven't quite developed your green thumb yet, there may still be hope for you. A nano garden is a way to grow all your own fruits, veggies, and herbs indoors without the help of sun or rain. It can automatically detect soil dryness and water the soil with the precise amount of moisture needed; in the

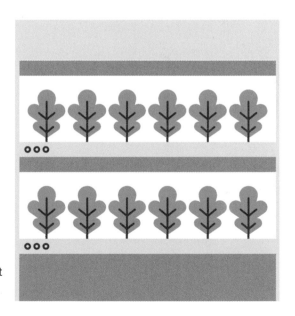

same way, it exposes plants with equal precision to faux sunlight. Guess we'll all be able to call ourselves farmers soon enough.

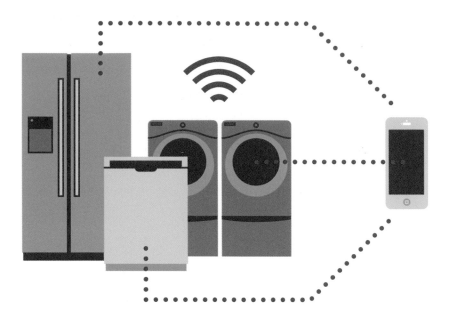

SMART APPLIANCES: Nearly every home appliance company (GE, Whirlpool, Viking, Samsung, etc.) is hard at work on embedding technology into everyday kitchen appliances like refrigerators, dishwashers, and stovetops. This is going to fundamentally change the kitchen as we know it. Once installed, these new appliances will come complete with Bluetooth and Wi-Fi functionality that lets them connect to both the web and your mobile devices to do things like send you alerts ("Dishwasher is done!" "Cupcakes are done!"), showcase virtual art (good-bye, refrigerator magnets; hello, PDFs?), and keep track of what's inside of them and message you accordingly ("Your milk is running low!" "Your leftovers have been refrigerated for over a week now").

3D FOOD PRINTERS: The Jetsons' reality is upon us. If you think 3D printers are cool, just wait until you see one that can print food. Several start-ups are already launching 3D food printers that can make edibles ranging from candy to cookies to pizza. Soon, they hope to have printers that let you make a much more diverse set of food with the touch of a button. Think about the implications of this invention!

TOUCHSCREEN APPLIANCES: Once appliances are able to connect to Wi-Fi, they will also be able to navigate and present information from the web. Imagine browsing your favorite food sites for recipes (for instance, www.brit.co/food), then pulling them up right on the surface of your stove as if it were a giant tablet. Experts say that these devices will also be able to suggest specific recipes based on the food they know you already have, ending the "there's nothing to eat" argument once and for all. (Unless there's really nothing to eat, in which case you should get to a grocery store or 3D food printer, stat.)

SMART SOUS-VIDE: If you have ever cooked using a sous-vide method, you probably know that it is one of the best ways to evenly cook a piece of food while keeping it incredibly moist. The technique, which has been around for a while, involves sealing the food in an airtight plastic bag, then submerging it in temperature-controlled water. Now a new company called Mellow has invented a device that does all the hard work for you. All you have to do is drop your food inside the machine, which can keep it chilled for as long as necessary, then will cook it in an instant once you instruct it to do so from an app on your phone. What's better is that it will learn your cooking preferences over time, eventually knowing exactly how you like your food cooked. It's like the most epic husband/chef combo ever.

DINING ROOM

The first word that comes to mind when I think about the dining room is conversation. Unless you're a dinner-in-front-of-the-TV type (I'm guilty of this on occasion too), this room is where you predominantly spend an hour or two at night, discussing the highs and lows of your day, catching up on life with family, and striking up conversations with friends.

The dining room is where you enjoy delicious fresh-from-the-oven meals, celebrate birthdays and holidays, and share stories and laughter.

But not everyone likes to play hostess. The most common reason for avoiding it is anxiety about making guests happy. It can be stressful to be responsible for keeping drinks topped, food warm, and guests entertained. Plus, there's the added joy of having to create a Pinterest-worthy tablescape that you hope your diners will ooh and aah over. Oh, and can you get that all done while also managing your work, errands, and kids?

It's no wonder we sometimes freak out about inviting guests over for a meal. Many of us lack the time to prepare and the knowledge to do it in the easiest way possible. We can't all be Martha Stewart or Suzy Homemaker, but we *can* learn a few simple ways to entertain in the dining room without getting stomach ulcers. Trust me, after adopting these methods myself, I can now throw together an epic dinner party in under an hour. Soon, you will too.

NOTES

Tips from the Co:

HAVE YOU SAID NO TO ELECTRONICS IN PARTS OF YOUR HOME OR DURING ACTIVITIES?

All phones go facedown, on silent, in the middle of the coffee table during hangouts with friends.

My husband and I both work full-time and have two kids under the age of four. We have a no-screens rule from the time we pick them up in the afternoon until they go to bed. We want to make sure the time we have with them at night is about them—not work or anything else.

When my daughter was little, we were broke. So, to save a little bit of cash, we had "No Electricity Wednesdays." No lights, no stove, no computers, etc. She loved these days and looked forward to them all week. She and I would talk and play board games. She learned to think about electricity and conservation. Even critical-thinking skills were learned. One night, when she was about six, we had a very serious discussion about why we should leave the fridge plugged in. Thank goodness she asked about it, rather than just fixing what she saw as a problem!

My balcony is a tech-free zone. I can go out there to read a book and briefly be away from the rest of the world.

My husband and I started a no-television-at-dinner rule. We used to eat dinner on the couch, and our dining room was covered in mail and bills and paperwork that needed attention. Now we eat dinner at the table. We talk to each other, and I believe our food tastes better.

No TV, computers, or "i" products (iPod, iPhone, etc.) on Friday nights—just pizza and board games.

I turn off our wireless router before I pick up my kids from school. I don't turn it back on until everyone is finished with homework.

How to Choose Glassware

Okay, guys, here's some real talk. Once you've graduated from college, it's probably best that you get rid of your red plastic cups. They aren't really the fanciest things to entertain with. Shocking, I know. If you have in fact made it to the next level of adulthood, you're probably pouring wine into a basic wineglass, beer into a tumbler (or drinking it straight from the bottle), and cocktails into God-knows-what.

But there are actually specific types of glassware made for specific types of drinks. While it should never be considered a "rule" to force your guests to drink out of them, it does make you look like you know what you're doing as a host or hostess when you can pour the proper drink into its proper glass. Here's the lowdown on all the glassware you need in your kitchen to look like a legit hostess with the mostess.

BEER   COGNAC   FLUTE   MARTINI

WHISKEY   COUPE   CORDIAL   MARGARITA

HOW TO CHOOSE WINE

Now that you have the correct glass chosen, let's pour some wine! If you're always getting stuck figuring out what to serve to your dinner guests, look no further than the humorous (but surprisingly accurate!) infographic on the next page. Keep it on hand for all of your upcoming dinner parties.

INVITATION ETIQUETTE

Gone are the days when Emily Post required you to send handwritten invitations and thank-you notes for every gathering you hosted. In today's world, digital invitations from online platforms like Paperless Post are much more commonly used and increasingly "approved" as adequate etiquette, especially among Millennials.

While I wouldn't necessarily send a digital invitation to a formal event like a wedding, doing so for dinner parties or birthday parties is completely A-OK. And in fact, it's probably much easier for both you and your guests to get reminders, send RSVPs, and see who else is coming.

Try to customize the wording and design of the invitations to make your invite unique. And if you have guests who aren't yet connected to the web (hello, Grandma), make a phone call to personally invite them to join the gathering.

WINE 101

everything you need to know about vino

SPARKLING	DRY WHITE	SWEET WHITE	RICH WHITE	ROSÉ	LIGHT RED	MEDIUM RED	BIG RED	DESSERT
Brut (dry)	Sauvignon Blanc	Riesling	Chardonnay	Old World (dry)	Pinot Noir	Merlot	Syrah	Port
Prosecco (sweet)	Pinot Gris	Gewürztraminer	Viognier	White Zinfandel (sweet)		Tempranillo	Malbec	Muscat
Sparkling Rosé (berry)						Zinfandel	Cabernet Sauvignon	Sherry
								"Late Harvest"

HOSTING A DINNER PARTY? SERVE WINE IN THIS ORDER →

serve ice cold   *serve cold*   *serve chilled*   *serve slightly chilled*

PROTEIN PAIRING

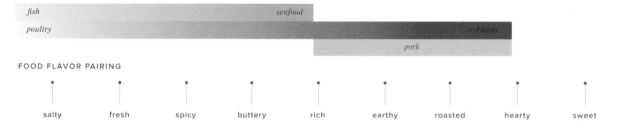

fish   *seafood*

poultry   *red meat*

pork

FOOD FLAVOR PAIRING

salty   fresh   spicy   buttery   rich   earthy   roasted   hearty   sweet

HOW LONG THAT OPEN BOTTLE WILL LAST

For best results, drink soon!

sparkling
2
DAYS

light red
2
DAYS

red
4
DAYS

white + rosé
7
DAYS

dessert
1
MONTH

HOW TO CHOOSE THE RIGHT GLASS

BIG BULB
for red

U SHAPE
for white

FLUTE
for sparkling

SMALL GLASSES
for dessert

HOW TO READ A WINE LABEL

The producer who made the wine. Some bottles highlight regions or blends here as well.

BRIT+CO

2011
PINOT NOIR
NAPA VALLEY
CALIFORNIA

750 ml   14% alc./vol

The year the grapes were harvested. Weather can affect the taste, so learn your favorite years!

The region where the wine is from.

The type of wine. Some bottles outside the US list region here instead, e.g. Red Burgundy = Pinot Noir.

Average bottle of wine contains 5 glasses (5 oz. pours).

Alcohol level. A higher number can mean bigger taste.

FIVE WAYS TO FOLD A NAPKIN

Napkin folding? Really, are we on a cruise ship?

The truth is, a few simple, origami-inspired folds are a quick and easy way to take your tablescape from ordinary to conversation-worthy. Take a cue from old-school hostesses with new-school tricks, patterns, and more colorful table linens. As far as how to make each design happen, I'll let the pictures do most of the talking.

UTENSIL POCKET

How convenient is that? This would be perfect for a less formal, picnic-inspired table setting. It would also be a cute way to keep utensils in order for buffet-style dining.

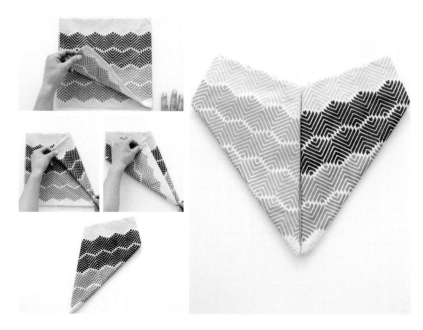

HEART

This one takes two napkins—it's sort of like those old "best friends" necklaces, but made of napkins! Yes, I just went there. This would be the sweetest way to display napkins for an impromptu romantic dinner for two.

ENVELOPE

I love the idea of using this option to hide a small gift or favor as a surprise for your guests. Depending on the type of event you are host-ing, you could put a photo, a personal note, or a business card inside.

BOW

This option requires a ribbon or napkin ring around the center. Naturally, I went with a 3D-printed napkin ring. That's right—I pressed one button to print out that bright turquoise geometric ring in less than ten minutes.

LOTUS

Finally, the mother lode of all napkin folding tutorials. This one requires not one, not two, but *four* napkins. It makes for a great centerpiece—though it's so pretty, you might not want to disassemble it! As you can see in the photos, it's similar to creating an old-school Fortune-Teller or Cootie Catcher, using napkins instead of paper. (You know you made those back in the day. We all did.)

THREE WAYS TO SET THE TABLE

When it comes to setting the table, I can definitely appreciate the formal, more traditional approach, but I personally tend to mix things up based on the type of gathering I'm putting together. If you're hosting a larger dinner party and aren't sure if people will end up sitting down or not, I recommend going with a picnic-inspired approach. Sort of like a buffet, but without the school cafeteria vibe.

FORMAL

Fancy up your table by going all out with the most formal of table settings. This scene is fit to suit royals, in-laws, and your best friends alike.

INFORMAL

This is the more standard, less formal table setting. While I still think it's formal enough to work for a dinner party or special event, it's less overwhelming, since it doesn't include quite so many glasses and utensils.

Tips from the Co:

HOW DO YOU SAVE TIME CLEANING YOUR HOME?

I wait until everyone else is gone and I plug in some upbeat tunes and bebop my way around the house. I'm finished before I know it (and before anyone can see my awesomely bad dance moves).

I do my big cleaning jobs on the weekend, and then I just have to do the light cleaning during the week. I also like to do bursts of cleaning and try to get as much done in 15–30 minutes as possible.

We put a timer on for 30 minutes, and everyone has to pitch in for the full half hour. After that, we are done, and anything left waits until the next day.

We have 15-minute cleanup frenzies where we see who can do the most cleaning in the time. I put on loud music, give everyone a basket and a rag, and set the timer. This is the perfect way to get the basic decluttering taken care of so I can get to the other chores like dishes and sweeping.

Note:
Only three people said that they hire a cleaner!

HACK: DECORATE WITH TEA TOWELS

Tea towels are a common product you can find at any home decorating store, but ironically, they are not always used for serving tea. In fact, I keep tons of these decorative towels around as a way to add color and function all around my kitchen. Here are two of my favorite unconventional ways to use 'em!

STYLE UP YOUR BREAD BOWL

Keep dinner rolls warm and stylish by lining your bread bowl or basket with a tea towel.

CARAFE WRAP

I love keeping ice water on the table, but I don't love all the condensation! Wrap your carafes or pitchers in a tea towel, almost like a scarf, to keep drips at bay.

Runner or tablecloth

Centerpiece

Place settings for all guests

Glasses

Napkins

Candles and votives

Bottle opener

Serveware

Wine opener

Cocktail shaker set

GADGETS AND APPS

AUTOMATED LOCKS: If you are frequently entertaining guests and hate dropping what you're doing to answer the doorbell, consider installing a smart lock like Kevo, August, or Lockitron. A smart lock makes it so that you can control who has access to your home, whether you are there or not. Enabled by your smartphone, a smart lock is unlocked with your visitor's phone. No key required.

DOORBOT: Okay, so maybe you don't want to give your guests smartphone-unlockable access to your home, but there are alternatives that make answering the door a bit more enjoyable. Doorbot is a way to see who is at your door, no matter where you are. So if you're running errands downtown, you can quickly catch a glimpse of who is stopping by, right when your visitor rings the bell. Your phone will alert you and share a live video. Have guests arriving early for dinner? Let them in with a quick tap of a button.

WIRELESS MUSIC STREAMING: Every gathering is made better with a bit of background music, and players like Sonos and Jambox make it very easy to stream music throughout large areas of your home. I use Sonos players everywhere in my house, so I can play party music in the kitchen and soft jazz in the bathtub. Because the app connects to your favorite music services (Spotify, Pandora, etc.), you never need to download them directly to your phone . . . meaning more storage space for all those Instagram pics.

DIGITAL INVITATIONS: As mentioned earlier in this chapter, digital invitations are definitely an approved way to invite guests over for a party or gathering. My favorite site is Paperless Post, though Evite and Punchbowl are also quite popular. If you're a web design master, you could also always opt to design an invite from scratch using Photoshop. Just attach the image file to your invite e-mail.

PHOTO EDITING APPS: No party is complete without capturing a few photos to remember it by. Hands down, my favorite photo editing apps are VSCO Cam, Camera+, and ProHDR. (ProHDR is the BEST for outdoor photos or photos taken in harsh light. Check out the #sunset pics in my Instagram feed to see what I mean.) And if you want to snag a pic of the entire group but don't want to leave anyone out, try HISY, a special app just for taking group selfies.

TO-DO LIST: Invites, food, table settings . . . what else? Are you forgetting anything? Clear is one of the best-designed to-do list apps out there. Try it during your next chaotic moment to "clear" that mind of yours.

DINNER DELIVERY SERVICES: Don't want to cook? Fake them out by making them think you're a pro chef. New services like Munchery deliver on-demand, chef-prepared meals to your door. All you have to do is plate them! Or if you want an *actual* chef to join your fiesta, try using a service like Kitchit, which lets you browse all kinds of local chefs who will come to your home and cook a multi-course meal for a fraction of what you might pay eating out.

Tip from the Co:
Put your smartphone in a bowl for natural sound amplification of music when you don't have easy access to speakers.

CUSTOM-ETCHED GLASSWARE

MATERIALS	GLASS ETCHING CREAM
	CONTACT PAPER
	VINYL LETTERS

TOOLS	SCISSORS
	PAINTBRUSH

I know what you're thinking. Etching glassware sounds like it could result in someone losing an eye. But the truth is, etching is super simple, takes only a few minutes, and can yield totally chic and customizable results. It's basically a way of frosting small-scale pieces of glass. For this project, I used contact paper to create custom designs or stencils. It's much more durable than painter's tape and allows for more creativity in terms of shapes and patterns. You can also use vinyl letters to etch labels into your jars and canisters for flour, sugar, rice, and so on.

STEP 1: Cut your contact paper into small shapes to create a pattern. I went with our signature triangle pattern on a glass carafe.

STEP 2: Wash and dry your glass carafe or pitcher to start out with a clean surface. Peel off the backing of your contact paper and attach each piece to the glass. Be sure to press firmly so that you get a clean edge when you start etching.

STEP 3: Use a paintbrush to apply a heavy layer of etching cream all over your carafe. Dab it on evenly, but don't brush too firmly, as that tends to thin out the cream. The thicker the layer of etching cream the better.

STEP 4: Let the etching cream sit for 30 minutes, then rinse it off with water. Be sure to clean your sink thoroughly after this rinse, as the etching cream is toxic.

STEP 5: Peel off your contact paper pattern and wipe with a damp towel or rag to remove any remaining traces of etching cream. Fill up with your favorite beverage and marvel at your handiwork.

I created a striped carafe, labeled a pitcher with the word PUNCH, and decorated a large Mason jar with the same triangle pattern. It's a great way to turn a bunch of mismatched glassware into a custom collection.

NOTES

COLORFUL
TABLE RUNNER

MATERIALS	FABRIC PAINT
	WHITE TABLE RUNNER
	(OR WHITE FABRIC
	HEMMED ON ALL FOUR
	SIDES)

TOOLS	PAINTER'S TAPE
	PAINTBRUSH
	IRON

If you're like me, you love to host your friends and family for dinner, cocktails, or brunch as often as possible. And even though there are tons of gorgeous table linens on the market, sometimes you just can't find what you want or don't want to end up spending more money than you'd like. However, with the right fabric paint and a plain white runner, you can create your own conversation-worthy piece of tableware in minutes.

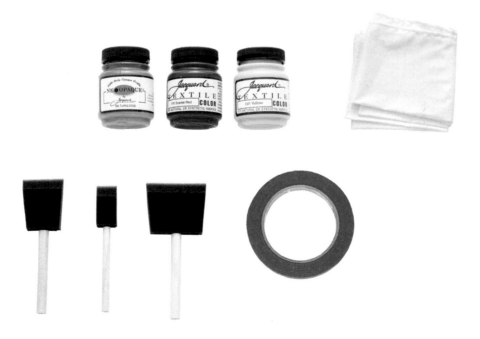

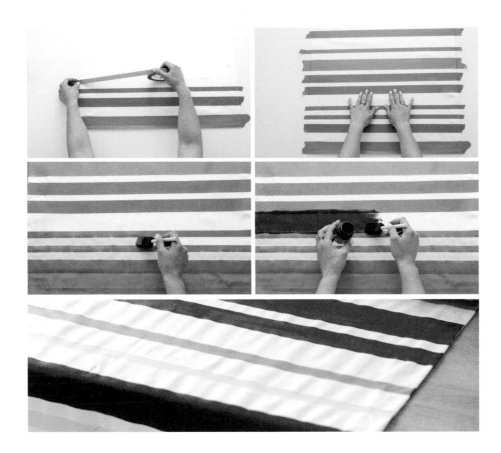

STEP 1: Iron your runner and lay it down on a flat surface. If you're creating a runner from scratch, simply hem all four edges and you'll be good to go. Start creating a pattern with painter's tape.

STEP 2: I created a striped pattern, with stripes that vary in thickness, inspired by the iconic striped Pendleton blankets (my fave blankets ever). Make sure to smooth out any air bubbles or puckers in the tape so that you end up with a clean paint line.

STEP 3: Start painting!

STEP 4: You may need to go in stages depending on how long your runner is and how big your worktable is.

Let the runner dry, then peel off the tape. I recommend washing, drying, and ironing your runner before placing it on your dining table. Next time you host a dinner party, you've got about 25 hostess points comin' your way!

NOTES

PATTERNED TEA TOWELS

MATERIALS	GOLD THREAD
	RED THREAD
	TEAL THREAD
	TEA TOWELS

TOOLS	SEWING MACHINE

This is one of my favorite decor DIYs. It's so simple, and it's a great way to get to know your sewing machine if you're just learning how to sew. You can buy basic flour-sack tea towels online or at pretty much any home goods store. Then it's all about picking the right thread colors and figuring out what crazy stitches and patterns your sewing machine can create. I made a set of three tea towels: one with basic stripes, one with squiggly patterned stripes, and one with a notebook-inspired pattern.

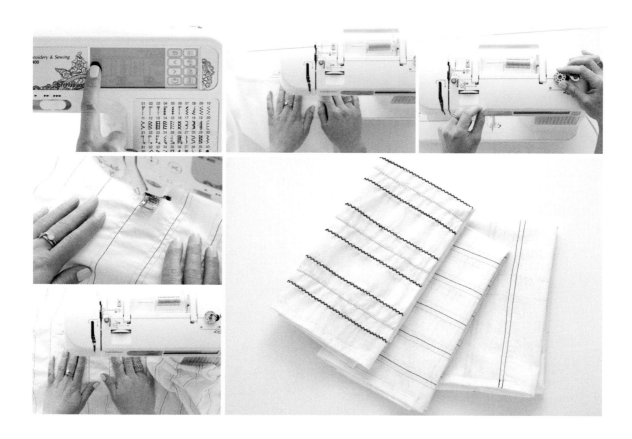

STEP 1: The best way to get started is to use a scrap piece of fabric to test out all the different stitches your machine has to offer.

STEP 2: Start at the right edge of your tea towel, with whatever color you like. I started things off with mint green and a pattern using a super-basic linear stitch.

STEP 3: When switching colors, be sure to switch your bobbin as well. Unlike typical sewing projects, this one is all about seeing the stitches on both sides.

STEP 4: Keep on sewing to get all those stripes in there.

STEP 5: And sewing, and sewing, and sewing . . . !

Make as many tea towels as you like. You can mix and match patterns or create a matching set. I love the idea of using this same method to create matching cloth napkins!

NOTES

BALLOON PHOTO BACKDROP

MATERIALS	FISHING LINE
	TAPE
	BALLOONS
	BALLOON PUMP

It should be no surprise that I'm obsessed with colorful photo backdrops. Whether creating a wall of color for the photo booth at a wedding or birthday party or simply throwing something up quick for a dinner party, this balloon wall is a great trick to know about.

The how-to for this is so darn simple! Get a bunch of balloons in a color palette that suits your event. Inflate them using a balloon pump, or ask your friends to help you blow them up. Attach the balloons to clear fishing line by tying a simple knot, then tape the fishing line to your wall. You may need a few pieces of tape per row of balloons, so clear tape will probably work best. Create as many rows as you like, and get ready to say cheese!

Though I love a beautiful floral arrangement, sometimes the big dramatic pieces don't work on your dining table. Maybe you need the extra real estate for dishes. Maybe you don't like the idea of people sitting across from each other with their faces blocked by giant flowers. Whatever your reason for wanting to mix things up, this hack is for you! Take a bunch of small vases, jars, or even glasses and bunch them together in the center of your dining table. Then simply pop flowers in them to create a centerpiece with a whole lot of dimension. No giant bouquet needed. How easy is that?

NOTES

PLATED CAKE STAND

MATERIALS	PLATES
	SOMETHING TO ACT AS A BASE—A CANDLESTICK, GLASS, OR BOWL WORKS WELL
	E6000 GLUE

This one takes a page right out of Modern Hostessing 101, if I do say so myself! With an assortment of materials and the right glue, you can turn pretty much any plate into a custom cake stand. In this case, I used different objects to create a white base: For one stand, I used a candlestick; then an upside-down mug for another; and three owl-shaped salt shakers for the third!

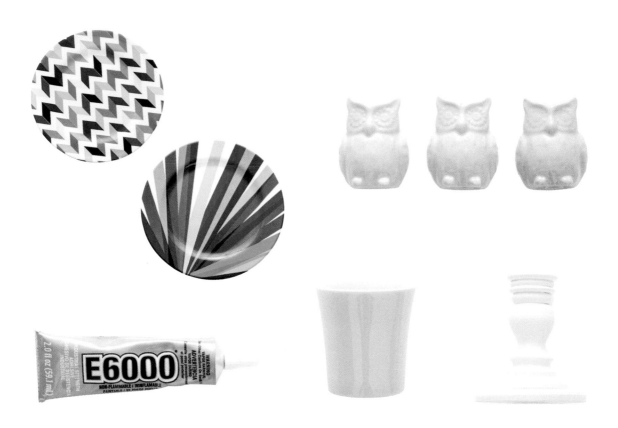

STEP 1: Squeeze E6000 glue onto the top of your base. This is where the plate will connect, so make sure to test your combination out beforehand to check that the plate balances.

STEP 2: Turn the base upside down and press it firmly onto the bottom of the plate.

You can follow the same process with a ceramic cup.

STEP 3: Be sure to let your cake stands dry overnight before using them. Then feel free to serve up cupcakes, macarons, and fruit tarts, oh my!

NOTES

FRINGE TASSEL GARLAND

MATERIALS	TISSUE PAPER
	STRING

TOOLS	SCISSORS
	HOT GLUE GUN AND
	GLUE STICK

You've probably seen a garland like this at a wedding, birthday party, or other festive event. But did you realize that it is actually pretty darn easy to make? I was inspired by the garland-makers at Studio Mucci (one of my favorite party design shops) to create this colorful project. It's an easy way to add an extra cheerful vibe to any event or gathering.

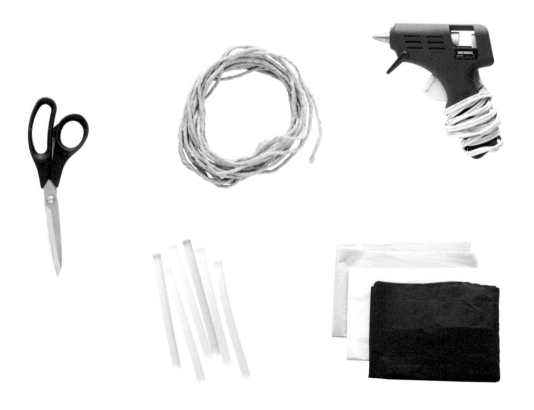

STEP 1: Layer three or four pieces of tissue paper on top of one another. Use scissors to cut the fringe pieces from the bottom, going about six inches up.

STEP 2: Keep going until you reach the edge of your tissue paper.

STEP 3: Roll up the tissue paper.

STEP 4: Twist the end right above the cut fringe to create a tassel.

STEP 5: Keep twisting the tissue paper until you can create a loop. Cut the tissue paper off once you have enough twisted to create a loop.

STEP 6: Use a hot glue gun to secure the loop at the top of your tassel. Now you've got one tassel!

STEP 7: Repeat this process until you've got a whole bunch of tassels, depending on how long you want your garland to be.

STEP 8: String them onto a piece of string.

STEP 9: And hang!

THE FUTURE DINING ROOM

Apart from those of you who will continue to text at the dinner table, this room is actually one of the few where technology will not necessarily play a large part over the coming years. Why is that? Because this room is focused on people and conversation, not on fancy apps or gadgets. It's one of the most social rooms in the house—the original social network!—and I for one hope it stays that way.

CONNECTED DINING TABLE: Imagine if your dining table and refrigerator had a baby. Some think that our future dining tables will contain a refrigerated core where we can easily store some of the foods we tend to eat and snack on most. (You know, because walking to a refrigerator might take too much energy.) I will say that the possibility of these tables including touchscreen surfaces does seem cool and appealing. Instead of eating cereal while holding up a giant morning newspaper, you might only have to flick your finger to turn the page.

GOODBYE, CHECKS: Asking for the check at a restaurant will soon be considered old school. In the near future, all of your financial information will be linked to your smartphone or other smart device you carry with you. A simple scan or wave of this device will pay your bill,

enabling you to leave at your convenience. And if it can do all of that, I'm willing to bet it can probably calculate the appropriate tip as well. Many restaurants are already starting to offer this functionality, so this trend may be mainstream before we know it.

INTERACTIVE MENUS: One other advance coming over the next few years will enable simpler and more efficient menu ordering at restaurants. Soon you'll be able to sit at your table, browse the menu through the tabletop display, and click on the things you'd like to order. The table may even tell you how much longer it will take before your food arrives, setting your hunger impatience at bay. Are the days of waiters and waitresses over as we know it?

NOTES

LIVING ROOM

If the kitchen is not the heart of your home, then the living room most certainly is. In fact, some still call it the "family" room, since it's the place where family members spend the most time together.

The living room is also one of the most adaptable rooms in the home. It can be used by one or many, and its purposes range from napping to book-reading, movie-watching, working, text-messaging, and entertaining.

To me, this is a room made for telling stories. Personal photographs lining the shelves or walls remind us of our favorite memories, and epic tales are told through the TV screen.

It's for these reasons that it's so important that the living room be a place where you can be comfortable for hours, whether you spend that time binge-watching your favorite shows or binge-chatting with your favorite people.

How to Decorate Without Spending Money

The living room is the one room you should pay the most decorative attention to, since it's where you spend the most time with the most people. If your budget isn't big enough to decorate your entire home, at least put your energy and dollars into creating a great living room.

But that doesn't mean you have to spend a lot of money. When it comes to redecorating with the furniture and decor you already have, just remember the Three Rs: Rearrange, Repurpose, and Restyle.

Rearranging your furniture in a new way will have a serious impact on your space. If anything, it will keep you from getting bored with your decor. See the layouts shown here to get a few ideas on how basic furniture can be repositioned in various ways to create an entirely new setting.

Decide how you intend to use your living room before deciding on a layout. If you and your family generally use the room for videos and entertainment, make sure that the furniture is facing the TV. If the living room is more of a social room for you, turn the chairs and couches toward one another to create a great platform for conversation.

4 LAYOUTS WITH THE SAME FURNITURE

Mix and match (and re-arrange!) your furniture depending on how you want to use your room. Here are a few ideas to get you started.

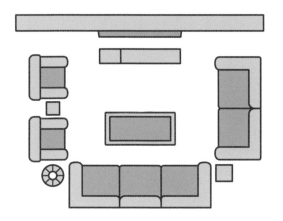

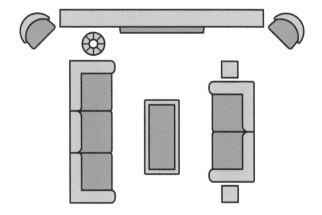

SMALL TALK: Okay for conversing, but most ideal for enjoying entertainment. All eyes are on the TV.

NEUTRAL: Couches face each other for direct conversation OR you can lay down to face the TV. Keep extra chairs in the corner in case of larger gatherings.

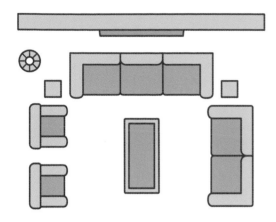

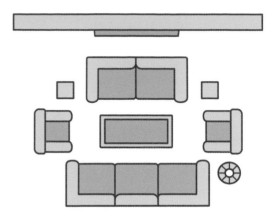

OPEN CONVERSATION: Furniture faces away from the fireplace and into the next room (likely the dining room or kitchen) to make it easy to gather and converse room-to-room.

DIRECT CONVERSATION: Intended for those who want to use the space for lots of chatting. (It also works well for multiplayer game nights!)

Repurposing your furniture is another inexpensive way to decorate (or redecorate) your home. Old wooden ladders can be transformed into shelves to display everything from books and magazines to blankets and towels. Also consider using found objects like old vintage suitcases or stacks of coffee-table books that can double as a side table, or try turning pallets from the flea market into a rustic coffee table. There are all kinds of ways to be creative while keeping chic.

Restyling—the final R of the Three Rs—is something I do nearly every month in my own home! I buy a ton of pillows, throw blankets, and accessories to mix and match as the seasons change. During the holidays, it's all metallics, greens, and reds. For summer, I love bold, bright colors. If you go this route, make sure to aim for neutral-colored furniture and rugs so that your accessories can really do the talking.

Tips from the Co:

HOW DO YOU REFRESH YOUR LIVING ROOM
WITHOUT BUYING ANYTHING NEW?

1. Rearrange

2. Paint the walls

3. Use accessories

I keep a box of framed art, tchotchkes, and throw pillows in my attic. When I get bored with the way things currently are, I rearrange furniture and trade out a few pieces I have for a few pieces in the backup box.

I keep my walls a neutral gray color so when I get bored with the decor I can literally do anything! I love using news clippings or magazine covers as framed art.

One of my favorite things to do is print out some small photos with an artsy filter. Then I create a border out of ribbon, washi tape, or paper and hang them on the wall above my desk or anywhere that needs a little inspiration.

Save some soda or tea bottles and paint them any color you'd like, but only on one side. (If you're in the mood for something more glamorous, you can use glitter.) These bottles are the perfect place to put little trinkets or fresh garden flowers.

HACK: SMALL-SPACE TRICKS

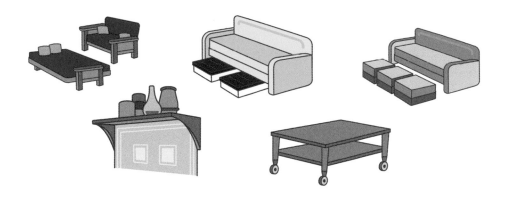

No space? No problem! I've had my fair share of tiny spaces to live in, from dorm rooms to studio apartments. Here are some tips and tricks for making the most out of your limited square footage.

When buying a sofa, look for one that doubles as a bed. If you live in a studio, serving as a bed will be the sofa's primary function, as you probably won't be entertaining too often in your small space. But in the event you have guests over, you'll definitely thank yourself for making sure they can sit somewhere other than where you sleep.

Shelving is clutch when you're short on space. Don't forget about the hidden places where shelves can also make an impact, like above the door. Take advantage of as much vertical space as you can!

It goes without saying that you should always create storage underneath furniture, whether a bed or a couch. Stock up on storage bins and baskets (ideally with wheels) to make it easy to access all of your stored goods.

If you often need more space to entertain friends, try putting some of your furniture on caster wheels so that it's easier to move things around quickly to make more room. Also consider an ottoman, which can double as a coffee table or a bench for extra seating.

Photo courtesy of Emily Henderson

Tips from the Co:

SMALL-SPACE TRICKS

EMILY HENDERSON

PROP STYLIST, *HGTV DESIGN STAR* WINNER, BLOGGER, AND NEW MOTHER

1. Use a tone-on-tone color palette. The more high-contrast colors you use, the busier the room can look, and therefore the smaller the room feels.

2. Use large mirrors to bounce around light as well as trick the eye into thinking the room is larger because of the reflection.

3. Get large-scale accessories, but fewer of them. You do not want lots of little things, as it will clutter the space.

4. Hanging your curtains at the ceiling rather than at window height will expand the visual size of the room and the window.

5. Use light-colored area rugs.

6. Use open shelving or glass-cased shelving instead of closed shelving to add depth and make the space look bigger.

THESE ARE THE TOP INTERIOR DESIGN MISTAKES MOST PEOPLE MAKE:

1. Having everything match, usually by ordering from a catalog and getting something right off the showroom floor

2. Scale issues—buying a huge couch or chair for a very small room

3. Hanging art at the wrong height

4. Using the wrong-size rug for the space

5. Scattering small accessories around the room rather than creating small vignettes or collections

Lamp

Couch

Art

Coffee table

Rug

Accessories

Chair

Side table

No interior designer? No problem. There are all kinds of apps and services for that.

APPS

HOMESTYLER: With this app, you can create a 3D image of your space so that you can clearly visualize how to lay out your furniture in different configurations.

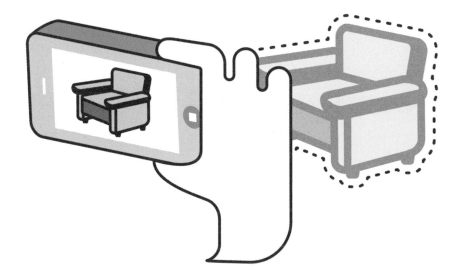

IKEA: IKEA's augmented reality app lets you point the camera of your phone at an empty space in your room, then drag and drop furniture into it to get a sense of how it will look. (Seriously, it's so cool.)

COLORCHANGE: This app virtually alters the colors of your walls and furniture to help you visualize what a new palette might look like. Just take a pic of the space and it'll work its magic. Shake to undo. Brilliant!

POLYVORE: Create mood boards of what you want your room to look and feel like, using images you find across the web. I seriously use this tool all the time, for everything from decor to fashion to event planning (like my wedding!).

PHOTO MEASURES: If you've ever had to use pencil and paper to sketch out a diagram of your walls so you can jot down measurements, then you will probably love Photo Measures, an app that digitizes the process. Instead of writing down your measurements on a paper diagram, you add them to a Photo Measure photo of the actual space. It's such a time-saver when you are hunting for furniture, frames, or appliances that will perfectly fit your room.

There's no lack of great apps to help you shop for furniture and home decor. Besides Brit + Co, my go-tos include One Kings Lane, 1st Dibs, and Craigslist (so many great scores there!).

SERVICES

ROOM IN A BOX was first touted by our girl Gwyneth Paltrow last year when she used it to make over her formal living room. Snap a few photos of a room that needs some love, and the service will pair you with interior designers who can make suggestions about layouts, furniture, and more.

DECORIST is a combination of Polyvore and Room in a Box. Not only can you take a quiz to help you understand your interior decor style  profile, but the app will let you create "boards" of rooms you might want to furnish. Decorist is also a community of interior designers who can do everything from consult with you to make over an entire room with you. This is a one-stop shop!

HOMEPOLISH takes the virtual interior design process to a whole new level. The service pairs you with a local designer who will come to check out your place in person for just $50. HomePolish then helps you decorate and renovate your space to your heart's content. You can work on projects of any size with this app, from styling art on a single wall to redecorating an entire home.

GADGETS

Most Americans own at least one TV, but as viewership of online video increases, smart TVs are becoming ever more popular. My favorite smart TV devices include:

CHROMECAST: This small device connects you to the HDMI port of your TV screen, which lets you broadcast all kinds of web video from the palm of your hand. (Literally the palm . . . you pair it with your mobile phone to select the videos you want to play.)

APPLE TV: Browse and watch everything from iTunes videos to Netflix videos.

KINDLE FIRE: Amazon's version of Apple TV. Tons of shows and movies to watch, plus access to Netflix and more. My favorite feature on this one is the ability to use your voice as the remote control.

MAC MINI: This is a device that essentially turns your TV into a computer. When connected to your TV display, it gives you the freedom to watch anything across the web.

GOOGLE TV: I actually helped launch this product a few years back! It gives you nearly full capability to watch video from across the entire web, since it has a built-in Chrome browser. It runs using the same Android operating system that your phone may use, so that you can also access apps that have been optimized for a big screen, from Pandora music to photo slideshows. I also use my smart TV devices to stream music, play games, or even showcase full-screen photos as art when I'm having guests over.

If you're a big video buff, be sure to invest in a set of great speakers to hook up to your entertainment system. While the cost of speakers can run the gamut, a decent set will set you back only a few hundred dollars. My husband would argue that it's totally worth it, but I personally don't always care about the sound quality of my movies. As long as I can hear it, I'm happy!

Gaming systems have come a long way since the days of playing Duck Hunt on Super Nintendos. In today's world, gaming devices can also function as smart TVs and are usually paired with a remote that uses gesture control (like a wave of the hand) to play the game. My personal favorite? Just Dance on the Wii—it's a game and a great workout all in one! Just be sure you're okay with looking a little silly in front of whomever you are playing with. Keep an eye on the gaming space over the next few years. Augmented reality goggles like the Oculus Rift will make gaming an even more immersive experience.

DIY PROJECTS

SEWING BASICS: DIY THROW PILLOWS

MATERIALS	COTTON FABRIC
	(NONSTRETCHY)
	INKJET TRANSFER PAPER
	THREAD THAT MATCHES
	YOUR FABRIC
	PILLOW STUFFING

TOOLS	FABRIC SCISSORS
	SEWING MACHINE
	INKJET PRINTER
	NEEDLE

If you're delving into the world of DIY, you've gotta learn a few sewing basics, and a simple throw pillow is a good place to start. But since a plain old pillow is a little too boring for me, I decided to add a custom iron-on design with three of my favorite words: MAKE, HACK, and LOVE. Come up with your own favorite words or phrase to add to your pillow.

Brit Tip:
*Use pillow
inserts that
are two inches
bigger than
your cover for
a fuller look.*

STEP 1: Measure your fabric and cut two pieces that are the same size. Here I went with 14-inch squares, which will result in 12-inch pillows.

STEP 2: Stack the two pieces on top of one another.

STEP 3: Now sew! You want to sew almost all the way around the perimeter, but it's essential to leave a two- to three-inch section unsewn so that you can turn it right side out, add the iron-on, and stuff it!

STEP 4: Turn your pillowcase right side out.

STEP 5: Use an iron to smooth out any wrinkles.

STEP 6: Print your iron-on transfer. Be sure to follow the directions on the package. Some inkjet transfer paper requires that you print in reverse (as you can see here), and some does not.

STEP 7: Iron the transfer onto your pillow.

STEP 8: Now it's time to make this pillow cozy. Fill it with stuffing or an insert until it's at a firmness that suits you.

STEP 9: Use a needle and thread to hand stitch the part of the pillowcase you left open.

And that's all! Now you just need to make enough pillows for a proper pillow fight!

GIGANTIC WOODEN WALL CLOCK

MATERIALS	CLOCK KIT
	PAINTER'S TAPE
	ACRYLIC OR HOUSE PAINT
	WOODEN CIRCLE
	VELCRO® BRAND TAPE
TOOLS	PAINTBRUSH

I'm all about functional wall art, and clocks are number one in that department. To create this spectacular clock, I combined a minimalist clock kit with a huge circular piece of wood. The result? Modern art meets time-telling awesomeness.

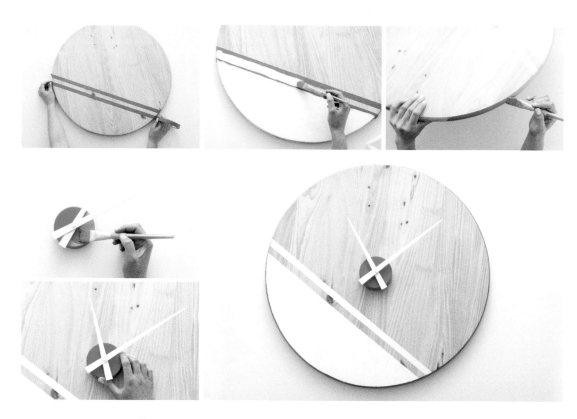

STEP 1: First, you want to prep your piece of wood. Use painter's tape to create a design. For this clock, I simply created two white blocks of color.

STEP 2: Paint the wood. Depending on what colors you're using, you may need two coats. Let the wood dry for an hour.

STEP 3: Paint the edge of your clock with a complementary color. In this case, I used deep teal on the edge. Let it dry for an hour.

STEP 4: Next it's time to paint your clock base and clock hands.

STEP 5: And finally, you need to place your clock on the wooden circle. Measure to find your center point.

STEP 6: Stick a piece of VELCRO® tape onto the center point as well as onto the back of your clock kit. You want the clock part to be removable so you can change out batteries as needed.

STEP 7: Attach the clock to your base, and that's it!

NOTES

STRING LIGHT CHANDELIER

MATERIALS	MINI-LANTERN STRING LIGHTS
	AQUA SPRAY PAINT
	STRING

TOOLS	NEEDLE-NOSE PLIERS

For this piece of statement lighting, I decided to mix things up. You've all seen pendant lights made of one big lantern, but what about a pendant light made of a whole bunch of little lanterns? And better yet, let's paint them ombre!

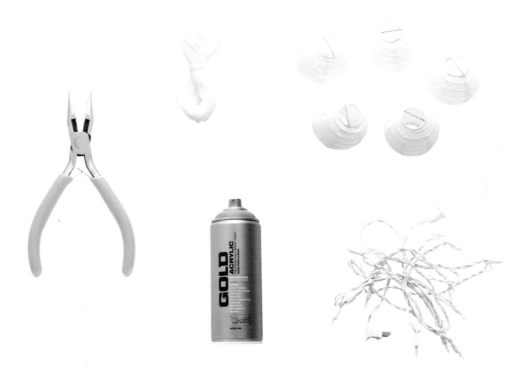

STEP 1: Depending on the mini-lantern kit you get, you might have to place a small metal piece in each lantern to help the lantern keep its shape. This is also how it will attach to the string lights.

STEP 2: Now let's paint those lanterns in an ombre fashion. I recommend using spray paint and starting at the bottom to create a more concentrated color. Then move up and lighten the pressure on the nozzle to create the ombre gradient effect. As with all spray-paint projects, it's best to do this outside due to the toxic fumes.

STEP 3: After your lanterns have dried, it's time to attach them to your string lights. You should be able to hook them right on.

STEP 4: I used needle nose-pliers to squeeze the metal hook area around each light to keep them more secure.

STEP 5: Then you simply bunch them together.

STEP 6: Use string to secure your lantern bundle. You may need multiple pieces of string to achieve the right shape.

STEP 7: If you want an extra spot of color, use electrical tape to wrap the hanging cord.

NOTES

PIXEL-PATTERNED COFFEE TABLE

MATERIALS	CONTACT PAPER IN A VARIETY OF COLORS WHITE COFFEE TABLE
TOOLS	RULER PEN SCISSORS

If you know the name of my dog, then you should know that I love pixels! (Spoiler alert: that's his name.) I also happen to love the ease of using contact paper to add a design to pretty much any flat surface. For this project, I'll show you how to use contact paper to create a pixelated pattern on a basic IKEA coffee table.

STEP 1: You'll have to choose the size of your square based on the size of your coffee table. In my case, I went with one-inch squares.

Draw a grid on the back of your contact paper.

STEP 2: Then cut 'em out!

STEP 3: Repeat with as many squares and colors as you like.

STEP 4: Lay the squares out on your table to decide on the design you want to create.

STEP 5: Once you have a design you like, it's time to start sticking those squares right on! Peel off the contact paper backing and attach each square to your table.

I recommend a random gridlike pattern, like you see here. If you want less color, this same method would totally work with just one or two colors.

NOTES

CONCRETE
SERVING TRAY

MATERIALS	CONCRETE MIX
	2 CABINET DOOR HANDLES
	CARDBOARD BOX
	(THE SIZE OF THE TRAY
	YOU WANT TO MAKE)
	WAX PAPER
	RED SPRAY PAINT

TOOLS	BUCKET FOR MIXING
	LONG WOODEN MIXING
	TOOL
	UTILITY KNIFE

Concrete is an affordable, sturdy material that adds a touch of industrial style to your home. For this project, I wanted to create a heavy tray that could sit on an ottoman or couch and act as a mobile coffee table for various accessories like magazines and drinks.

STEP 1: You know I can't resist a pop of color! In this case, I decided to spray-paint the door handles bright red.

STEP 2: Now you need to prep the box before you pour the concrete into it. Cut off the flaps that close your box. Reserve one.

STEP 3: Cut the box down to about an inch higher than how deep you want your tray to be.

STEP 4: Because the box I used wasn't flat at the bottom, I used one of the flaps I cut off to create a more even base.

STEP 5: Line the box with wax paper.

STEP 6: Now mix up your concrete according to the instructions on your concrete package.

STEP 7: Pour concrete into the wax-paper-lined box.

STEP 8: Place the red door handles in the concrete at either end. Let harden overnight.

STEP 9: Pull your tray out of the box.

STEP 10: Peel the excess wax paper off the bottom. And you're done!

CHIC SHAG OTTOMAN

MATERIALS	THICK WHITE YARN
	STANDARD WHITE YARN
	OTTOMAN

TOOLS	HOT GLUE GUN
	SCISSORS

I love the trend of shaggy poufs or ottomans, but I don't love the price tag that often accompanies them. So, time to hack! In this project, I'll show you how to turn a summer camp craft classic (pom-poms!) into a chic piece of decor for your home. Just find a used or affordable ottoman and some yarn!

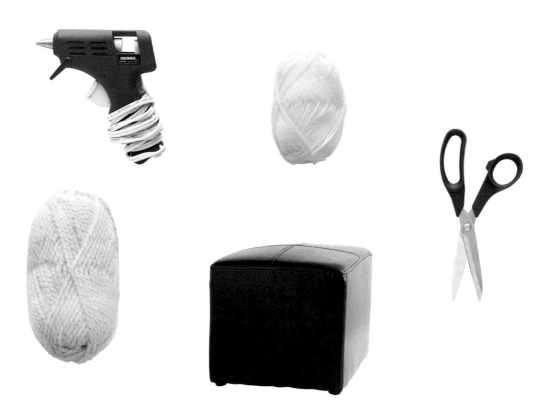

STEP 1: The first thing you need to do is create a whole bunch of pom-poms. Wrap yarn around your fingers like you see in the photo.

STEP 2: Keep wrapping until you've got a layer that's almost an inch thick.

STEP 3: Slide the yarn off your fingers carefully and cut off an extra piece of yarn to tie around your bundle.

STEP 4: Tie a piece of yarn around the bundle across the middle. Tie it really, really tight!

STEP 5: Now cut the loops! You want to cut them along the top so that they are all around the same length.

STEP 6: Once all the loops are cut, trim off any extra-long pieces that might be sticking out.

STEP 7: Keep making pom-poms until you've got a few boxes' worth.

STEP 8: Bunch them up to see how many more you need to make and whether you need additional thick or thin ones.

STEP 9: Use a hot glue gun to attach them to your boring old ottoman.

It's as simple as that!

STEP 10: Keep going until you've covered the whole ottoman.

And poof, you've got a pouf!

HACK: CREATE A SALON WALL

As someone who tends to collect a lot of art without always planning ahead, the salon wall is one of my favorite interior design hacks. It's an easy way to create a collage of things that don't necessarily go together, and you can keep adding to it after you've hung the initial collection of art. You can mix personal photos, postcards, and fine art all together as long as you follow a few simple rules.

1. Choose frames that go well together. I chose all white for this scene, but you can mix and match colors so long as nothing stands out too much.

2. Avoid going too symmetrical. You don't want a center image that is surrounded by the same number of images on each side.

3. Don't be afraid to mix quirky with beautiful! The great thing about this type of gallery style is that you can group pretty much anything together.

JERSEY-KNIT MACRAMÉ HANGING PLANTERS

MATERIALS	JERSEY-KNIT FABRIC (1 YARD PER PLANTER) PLASTIC OR CERAMIC PLANTER OR BOWL
TOOLS	RULER FABRIC

What's the first thing you think when you hear jersey knit? Old T-shirts! No, I'm not suggesting you finally hand over your Britney tour merch from the late '90s, but I am recommending that you take stock of all the unworn or completely worn-out T-shirts crowding your closet. If you don't have T-shirts, jersey-knit material is easy to come by at any fabric store, and you don't need much to make these!

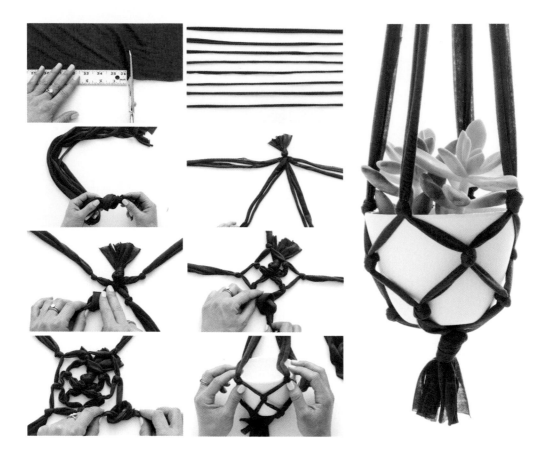

STEP 1: Cut eight pieces of material that are three to five feet long, depending on how long you want your planters to hang.

STEP 2: Tie a knot on one end, leaving the excess material at the top like a tassel.

STEP 3: Lay out your rope in four sections (like a cross shape), with two pieces of rope per section.

STEP 4: About an inch and a half down, tie a knot into each section.

STEP 5: Arrange your fabric so that it's once again in a cross shape. For this next part, knot fabric together from adjacent segments.

STEP 6: Once you're done with that, arrange your fabric yet again into a cross shape. And—you guessed it—knot material together from adjacent segments.

STEP 7: Slide your planter into the macramé net–like pouch you've created. And you're done!

NOTES

HACK: USE WASHI TAPE TO MAKE FAUX WALLPAPER

This has become one of our favorite go-to decor hacks around the Brit + Co office. If you've got an empty wall that needs a little color love, all you need are a few rolls of washi tape to make your own mural. I recommend using three to four types of washi tape—intricate patterns don't always show up when you're working with a large surface area. You simply tape onto the wall, and keep going until you've got a design you like. When you're bored with it, peel it right off. Washi tape is paper-based, so it peels off easily and won't ruin your wall.

THE FUTURE LIVING ROOM

TVS: The tech world can't stop talking about the future of TV. The hype of smart TVs and 3D TVs is still around, but the most interesting new conversation is about bendable TVs. These devices can switch from a flat screen to a bent screen in seconds, giving you an even more immersive watching experience.

WALLS: True story: When I was in college, I debated studying nanotechnology because I was so certain that a world of color-changing, LED wallpaper was coming soon. Turns out, I was right. 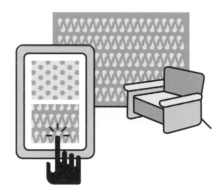 Wallpaper is having a major moment right now owing to scientists' advances in making technology parts tinier and tinier. Just as your

Kindle can display a page of a book, soon your wall will be able to display a solid or patterned color that you can change with the touch of a button. Even cooler? Your walls will also soon be able to display digital photos, tweets, videos, and more. Every surface of your house could one day become digitized and customizable. Imagine going to bed and looking at your ceiling that has transformed into a starry night! Crazy.

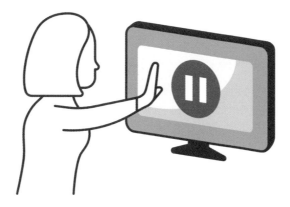

GESTURE-CONTROLLED TECHNOLOGY: Prepare to tell your children about the history of remote controls. We won't be needing them much longer, now that devices are being built with gesture-controlled technology. Want to pause the video? Just hold your hand up like a stop sign. Wave your hand to the right twice to fast-forward. There's no telling what continuous improvements in this space might mean, but I for one am excited about the fact that this tech advancement is likely to decrease the rate of carpal tunnel syndrome in humans. Now if only we could get rid of our computer mouse, too . . .

VOICE AND FACE RECOGNITION:

Just as you'll soon be able to control your devices with gestures, your devices will also be able to detect *who* is controlling them. That's right, new sensors are being developed that can recognize a voice or face, making it so that  all of your gadgets and gizmos, personalized to your settings, recognize you as soon as you walk in the door. Love pop music? In the future, you might return home to your living room with Justin Timberlake playing in the background, the lights dimmed to your custom settings, and the A/C turned down exactly the way you like it.

GAMING AND VIRTUAL REALITY:

Last year Facebook acquired a company called Oculus Rift, which has created a new immersive gaming experience. Just put on a set of goggles and you will feel like you have been instantly transported somewhere else in the world. The technology will  soon be so advanced that these goggles may provide you with not only a fun way to play games but also a way to watch movies, virtually attend live concerts, travel abroad (without the skyrocket plane fares), or even virtually shop at your favorite stores.

NOTES

BEDROOM

So many people think their bedrooms are unimportant, yet it's where we spend about a third of our lives. Shouldn't it be as comfortable as possible? All too often, I see bedrooms with cluttered walls, floors, and disheveled beds. I'm not saying your bedroom has to be as pristine as a five-star hotel room, but I do think it should be the calmest and most relaxing room in the home.

Choosing the right mattress and sheet set is a great first step, but there are also all kinds of other easy ways to keep your room clutter-free and sleep-ready. And please, keep those sheets washed. According to a survey, most single women wash their sheets every two and a half weeks and most single men wash theirs every twelve weeks. That's nearly three months . . . or just four times per year—yuck! The good news is that once you're in a relationship, the odds are that you will wash your sheets at least once every two to three weeks. Just another reason to seek out true love.

WHY IS SLEEP SO IMPORTANT?

Did you know you'll sleep for a total of about 32 years during your entire lifetime? And yet, most people in today's modern society are sleep deprived. Russell Foster, a circadian neuroscientist (whoa, that's a cool-sounding occupation), has been studying sleep for years, specifically researching its impact on our brains. He has found that those who get the proper amount of sleep (ideally eight hours per night—most of us are sleeping only six and a half hours per night) are three times better at decision-making, which leads to greater creativity and concentration, better social skills, and improved health. Another interesting finding is that those who get five hours of sleep or less per night are 50% more likely to be obese, as a sleep-deprived body tends to crave carbs for more energy. To get the best sleep possible, Dr. Foster suggests reducing your light exposure at least half an hour before going to bed, turning off all devices, cutting off caffeine early in the day, making your room slightly cool, and sleeping in as dark a room as possible.

HOW TO MAKE YOUR BED USING HOSPITAL CORNERS

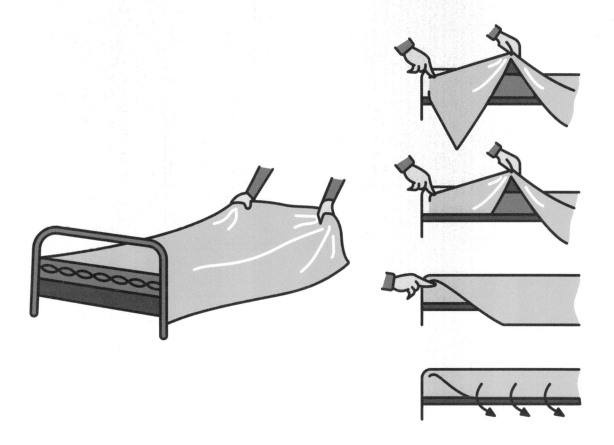

If you're constantly frustrated about your sheets coming untucked at night, you probably aren't utilizing the age-old trick of hospital corners. It's simpler than you think and will keep you snug as a bug in a rug.

HOW TO FOLD A FITTED SHEET

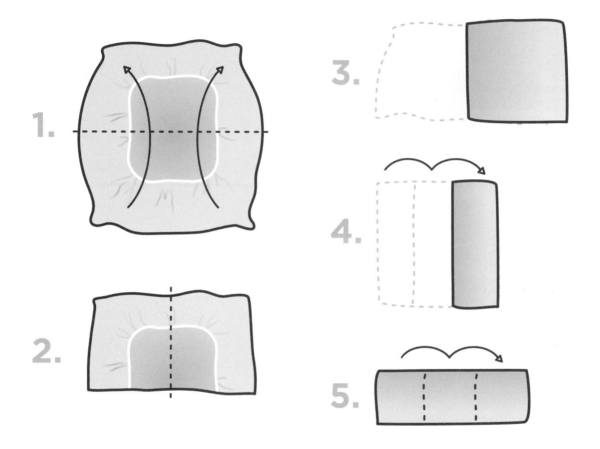

It's shocking how many people still don't know this trick! Practice it a few times and you'll be a sheet-folding expert. Tip: Once all your sheets are folded, tuck them inside of a pillow sham to group them together for storage in your linen closet. This is a helpful way to keep your bed sets organized.

If you want your bedroom to be calmer, think about using quieter colors like blues, lavenders, and greens in addition to symmetry, which balances out a room and makes it a less fussy space for relaxing in at the end of the evening.

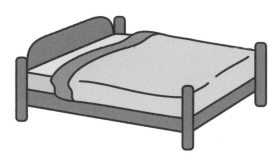

Mattress and sheet set

Art or wallpaper

Bedside table

Bed frame

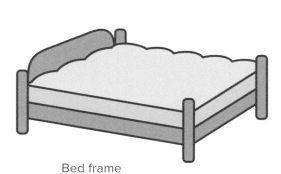

Accessories

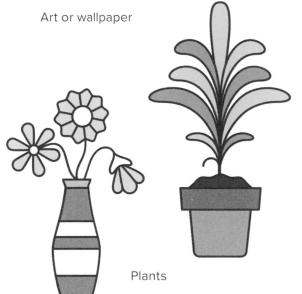

Plants

SLEEP TRACKERS: Connected sleep trackers can tell you exactly how many zzz's you're getting and how high-quality they are. The gadget works by putting a thin sensor under your mattress that can feel the rise and fall of your chest and how often you toss and turn. It then uses that data to understand your sleep cycles throughout the night. The sensor also pairs with an ambient light that naturally wakes you up at the appropriate time of light rest every morning, making sure you never have a groggy wake-up sesh again.

AUTOMATED LIGHTS: All things in our homes are becoming "connected"—even our lights! Lightbulb manufacturers have created bulbs that can turn on, off, or dim on demand . . . right from your phone. Some, like Phillips Hue, even have apps that let you modify the light color on the fly. And some are programming their lights to detect your presence in a room, thus signaling the lighting to change to match your preference.

SMART AIR CONDITIONING: If you don't yet have a Nest thermostat, you need one immediately. It's a life changer. The Nest works by letting you program your thermostat from wherever you are. All you have to do is open the app on your phone. If you're away from home, keep the A/C off; if you're freezing in bed at night, simply turn up the heat with a couple taps of a button.

ALARM CLOCK APPS: There are all kinds of useful (and silly) alarm clock apps you can download these days, from those that are simply beautiful, like UNIQLO Wake Up, to those that are a bit more forceful in the morning. Both Walk Up and Walk Me Up, for instance, make you get out of bed and walk around to turn them off.

WHITE NOISE APPS: If you have a snoring bedtime partner, consider downloading a white noise app that will drown out the sound. There are tons in your phone's app store that would be a great fit.

BEDROOM

DIY PROJECTS

GADGET-CHARGING NIGHTSTAND

MATERIALS	WOODEN NIGHTSTAND VELCRO® BRAND TAPE WIRELESS CHARGING MAT
TOOLS	ROUTER E6000 GLUE

You read that title right. In this project, we'll take a basic nightstand and turn it into a bedside table that wirelessly charges your handheld devices. All you need is a charging mat that is compatible with your smartphone or tablet, access to a router (hello, Woodshop 101!), and the right table.

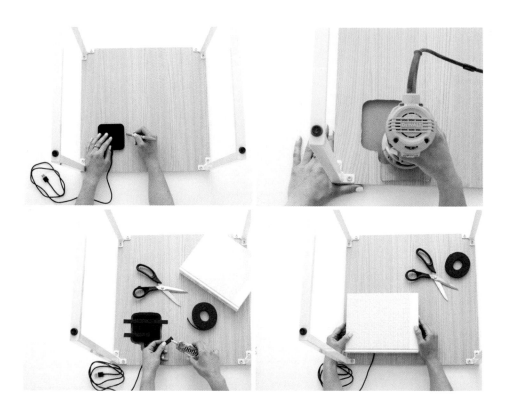

STEP 1: Turn your nightstand or table upside down. This is where you'll be attaching the charging mat. Trace the charging mat so you know what size indentation you need to carve out.

STEP 2: Use your router to carve out the shape you just traced. If you've never used a router, get ready for a whole lot of sawdust to come out. Be careful not to go through the whole nightstand—you just want to create a little pocket for your charging mat.

STEP 3: Now you need a way to keep that router in place. I used VELCRO® tape in my favorite color—red! Cut four pieces so that they attach in the middle and it's easy to take out the charging mat if need be. Use E6000 glue to attach the tape to the nightstand.

STEP 4: Place a heavy book over the glued tape to make sure it attaches securely to the table. Let it dry overnight. Plug the charging mat into the wall and you've got a table that charges your smartphone wirelessly!

EASY DYED PILLOWCASES

MATERIALS	CONTACT PAPER
	SPRAY DYE
	PILLOWCASE

TOOLS	SCISSORS
	CARDBOARD

For this next trick, I'll show you how to add a punch of color, pizzazz, and personality to your pillowcases. Unlike fabric paint, which can leave a less-than-snuggly rough finish, spray dye actually dyes the fibers of the pillowcase—that means the fabric will stay soft. The nice thing about spray dye is that you don't have to boil all sorts of crazy chemicals to dye materials. It's way less messy. (Anyone who has ever tie-dyed before will totally understand what that means.) You just need an open area to spray in! In terms of patterns, you can use painter's tape to create stripes or contact paper to create more intricate patterns. I went with the Brit + Co signature triangles to create a geometric look.

STEP 1: Spray dye works best on smooth materials without any texture. Once you've ironed and prepped your pillowcase, set it aside and take your scissors to that contact paper to cut out triangles—or any other shape you like!

STEP 2: Peel off the contact paper backing and adhere the triangles to your pillowcase. I created a pattern that starts out with lots of triangles at the bottom, then peters out toward the top of the pillowcase.

STEP 3: Place your pillowcase on a drop cloth or newspaper to catch any dye that goes off the edges of the pillowcase. Slide a piece of cardboard into the pillowcase so you don't dye through to the back. Hold the spray bottle eight to ten inches away from the pillowcase and spray to cover the entire thing.

STEP 4: Let the pillowcase dry for a couple of hours. Peel off the contact paper and pat yourself on the back for a job well done.

STEP 5: Then lay your head down and dream of creative ideas, playful patterns, and '90s heartthrobs.

Tips from the Co:

WHAT WAS YOUR BEST "I DIDN'T BUY, I DIY'D" MOMENT AT HOME?

I upholstered our basic black IKEA Lack coffee table when we needed to baby-proof our home. I added about a foot of foam to the top, cut off the bottom of the legs to keep the height the same, and spray-painted the bottom shelf and legs to match the fabric.

I turned an old thrift-store picture frame into a headboard. I spray-painted the frame and covered the old painting with batting and fabric. An afternoon and $20, and I have something uniquely mine and perfect for my home.

I modernized an antique carved dresser by removing its doors and slapping on some charcoal paint. The final result looked like it belonged at a high-end furniture store!

I recently came across a fur throw blanket in a home wares store I just fell in love with, but because of the $200 price tag I knew it wouldn't be mine. However, after a trip to the fabric store with vouchers in hand, I found the exact same fur, got some backing fleece, and $40 and two hours later I had my throw.

I made end tables made from old books that I drilled together with a glass round top.

I covered the old, yellowed refrigerator in our apartment in graphic black-and-white contact paper. It's a showstopper that every visitor comments on.

FABRIC STRIP CURTAIN

MATERIALS	JERSEY-KNIT MATERIAL
	CURTAIN ROD
TOOLS	FABRIC SCISSORS

Who says a curtain has to be made with a single piece of fabric? You can get the same look by cutting several fabric strips and weaving them together, for a more bohemian vibe. This project, which is all about choosing a color palette that suits your style, could also make for a great headboard alternative.

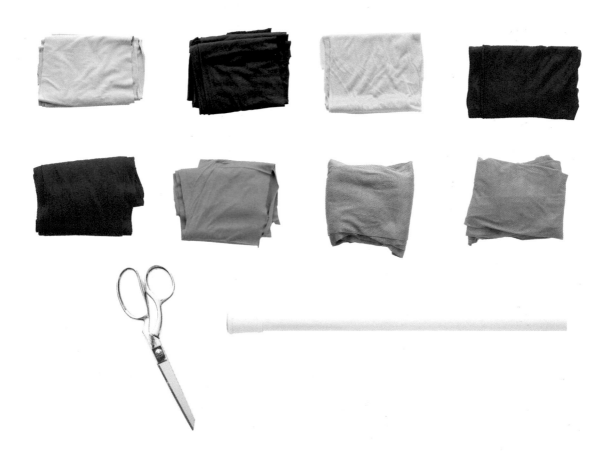

STEP 1: The most labor-intensive part of this project is the cutting, cutting, and more cutting! Sharpen up those fabric scissors and cue up your favorite rom-com for this part. I used strips that were three to four inches wide and made them a bit longer than my window. The great thing with this type of material is that they don't have to be perfectly cut to look good. In fact, a little variation can actually enhance the boho style.

STEP 2: Keep on cutting those strips of fabric. Organize them into piles by color.

STEP 3: Once you've got as many as you need, tie loops at the top.

STEP 4: Simply slip them onto a curtain rod in whatever color arrangement you like. That's it!

This would also make for an amazing photo booth backdrop. You know I love any DIY that can be used for more than one thing!

THE FUTURE BEDROOM

SLEEP IQ: Mattress manufacturers are developing sleep trackers within their springs that can give incredibly accurate readings on your sleep quality, based on how often you toss and turn and how deeply you breathe. These new high-tech mattresses might cost you a pretty penny, but isn't that worth the price of a healthier life?

HEAT-REACTIVE MATTRESSES: Not only will your future mattress be able to collect data on how well you're sleeping, but it might even help you sleep better, especially if you often get too hot or too cold at night. Some companies are now using cutting-edge optical fibers and copper yarns that are knit into the fabric of a mattress to sense whether a sleeper is too hot or too cold. At that point, the mattress can either give off heat or create a cooling effect on the skin, keeping the sleeper at a perfect temperature the entire night.

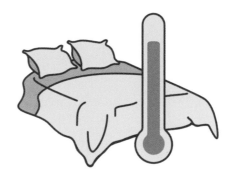

CONDUCTIVE INK POSTERS: If you have posters adorning any of your bedroom walls, you might be interested to know that the posters of the future will be used not only for decorating but also for playing music and generating  smells. That's right—new conductive ink posters generate sound and aroma when you touch them. Now there's a reason to believe that "print" will never die.

GRAPHENE: A new form of carbon, graphene, is 200 times stronger than steel yet so light that it can land on a blade of grass without bending it. There are myriad uses being formulated for this material, one of 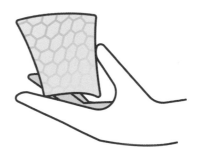 which will be to interact with your body's sleep system. Understanding when you have fallen asleep, it will be programmed to dim the lights in your home and turn off all devices, and then it will start up the coffeemaker as soon as it knows you've woken up.

SMART GLASS: If you aren't a big fan of curtains but are increasingly concerned about privacy (especially in the bedroom, where some things should be, well, private), consider installing smart glass, a type of window glass that can be controlled by electricity. Your windows can then be turned from transparent to translucent with the flick of a switch. The glass can also block ultraviolet light, saving you mega-bucks on heating and cooling.

CLOSET

The closet is either a woman's favorite place in the house or the space she most abhors. Getting dressed is a ritual, and frankly, women either love it or hate it—or most often, both! "What will I wear?" "Why is this not fitting right?" "Do I look fat?" "I have nothing in here!"

Too often, women will splurge on new clothes either because they're bored and don't realize how to make old clothes seem new again, or because they aren't buying clothes that fit them properly in the first place and thus grow to dislike them over time. Granted, most women simply find it fun to go shopping for new and fabulous things, but the next time you hit the mall, make sure you think about the real rationale behind your credit card extravaganza. The second most common problem people face with getting dressed is not knowing what they have to work with. I personally try to avoid drawers and bins at all costs, except for basic garments like underwear and socks. The more options you can see at once, the more creative you can be with mixing and matching your wardrobe in stylish ways. Read on to learn how to turn your love-hate relationship with your closet into a full-on romance.

Closet Organization 101

SUPPLIES

LABEL MAKER
BINS, BASKETS, AND BOXES
CLOTHES

While organizing your clothes isn't always the most fun task in the world, it will save you a ton of time in the morning and enable you to dress more creatively because you'll be able to see all of your options at a glance. Here are my personal tips and tricks for keeping that closet in check.

WHAT TO FOLD, WHAT TO HANG

I am admittedly a type A closet freak. I love to have everything super-organized, yet out where I can see it. If I can't see it, I usually forget about it. Thus, here are some rules for things to fold and things to hang.

Tip from the Co:
Use shower ring/ hooks on your closet rod for an easy way to hang and display scarves and bags.

FOLD
Undergarments
T-shirts
Jeans
Athletic apparel
Sweats/loungewear
Sweaters

HANG
Everything else

Tips from the Co:

If you haven't worn it in a year, throw it out! The best organization is not having to struggle through junk to find what you really love.

Use the back of a door to maximize space. Add small hanger hooks for grab-and-go items (i.e., a jacket, scarves, etc.).

Amortize. Buy quality things that will last a long time. Say no to cheap fashion. When you do that, you'll end up with fewer things and a cleaner closet.

I go to local thrift shops and buy vintage suitcases to store winter clothes up high on shelves without the "clutter" look that usually comes with stacking piles of sweaters. They cost just a few dollars (I bought three vibrantly colored ones for $5 once!) and can hold a whole lot of sweaters! Bonus: They don't smell like mothballs and are within easy reach on a chilly summer beach night.

Most women (and men!) don't realize how important tailoring is, or where their clothes should be tailored. Once done properly, not only will a tailored piece of clothing bring out your best bodily features, but it will become a piece you wear over and over again because it fits just right. Here are the most common rules for tailoring your clothes:

 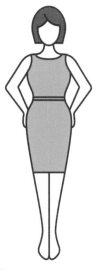 

ANKLES

Hem just below the ankles if you primarily wear flats, and make hems one to two inches longer for pants you often wear with heels. When in doubt, leave the pants longer and roll up or fake a hem with a couple of safety pins when needed.

WAIST

Show off that waist, girl! Tops and dresses that are hemmed close to the waist help you appear leaner and curvier. Pear-shaped women should especially focus on showing off this part of their body, as it's their best asset.

SHOULDERS

The top sleeve seam of your tops should always sit squarely at the edge of your shoulder—not further inside and not further down your arm.

If I could give one piece of advice to women that would help them to dress themselves better, it would be to understand what body type they have. Here are the most common shapes:

 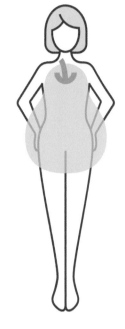 

APPLE

Apple-shaped women have broader shoulders and bust and narrower hips.

BANANA OR STRAIGHT

Banana-shaped women's waist measurement is less than nine inches smaller than their hip or bust measurement.

PEAR, SPOON, OR BELL

Pear-shaped women's hip measurements are greater than their bust measurements.

HOURGLASS

Here the hip and bust are almost of equal size, with a narrow waist.

A study of more than 6,000 women conducted at North Carolina State University in 2005 revealed that 46% of them were banana-shaped, just over 20% were pear-shaped, just under 14% were apple-shaped, and only 8% were hourglass-shaped. The hourglass is normally accepted as the "ideal" female shape in Western countries.

DRESSING IN THE RULE OF THIRDS

DO:

DON'T:

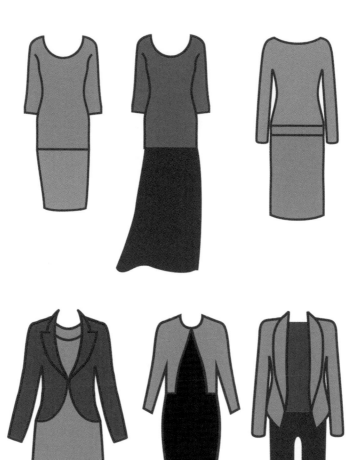

The "Rule of Thirds" is a good way of making sure that the outfit you're wearing accentuates your body as best it can. As you can see from the illustrations, you want to be sure that you're emphasizing either your top third or your bottom third. Try not to wear a half-and-half style, or you will cut off some of your best features.

White button-down shirt

Jeans
(skinny, boot cut, and relaxed)

Blazer

Belt

Sandals

Little black dress

Proper-fitting bra

Undies

Booties

Scarf

Basic T-shirt

Sweater

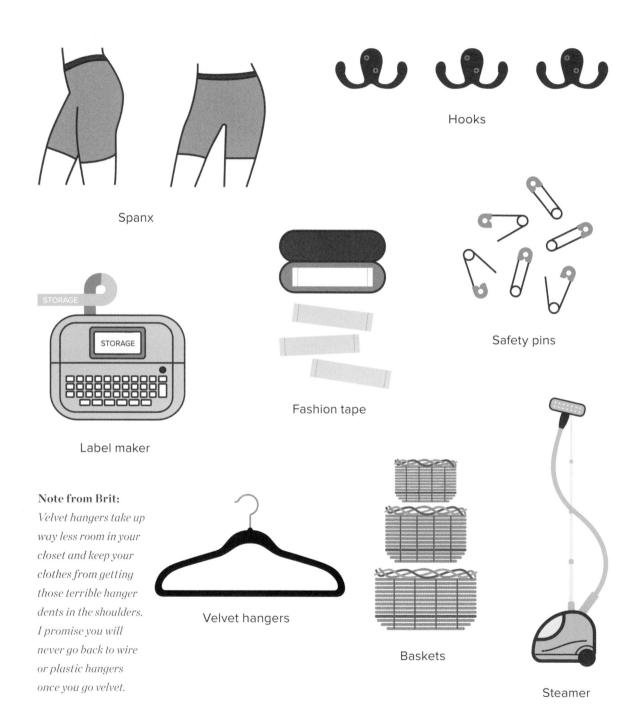

Spanx

Hooks

Label maker

Fashion tape

Safety pins

Note from Brit:
Velvet hangers take up way less room in your closet and keep your clothes from getting those terrible hanger dents in the shoulders. I promise you will never go back to wire or plastic hangers once you go velvet.

Velvet hangers

Baskets

Steamer

NOTES

5 WAYS TO STYLE A SCARF

Scarves are so ridiculously versatile—you can wear them around your neck, in your hair, as a vest, or even as a bag. Here are five scarf hacks every woman should know.

LOOK 1

FAUX INFINITY SCARF:
I love the trend of circle or infinity scarves, but don't love how limited you are when you buy one readymade. Take the two ends of any standard scarf and tie in a knot. Boom! You've got a brand-new circle scarf.

LOOK 2

SCARF VEST: This is one of my all-time favorite fashion tricks, and it also involves some clever knotting. Fold your scarf in half. Tie one folded corner with one end corner, and you magically have a racer-back vest. Amazing, right?

LOOK 3

BOHO BELT: This simple trick is a great way to personalize a basic T-shirt and jeans ensemble. Roll up your scarf as thin as it will go, then loop it through your belt loops. I like tying it on one side and tucking away the extra scarf length, but you could also rock a big floppy bow on the side.

LOOK 4

SLOUCHY BAG: Lay your scarf out on the floor. Depending on how wide it is, you might want to fold it in half. Starting from the center, measure two or three hands' length out. Then tie a knot. Do the same on both sides. You should have a little pouch now! To finish things off, tie the two ends together to create a strap.

LOOK 5

HEADBAND: Finally, take the turban and thick headband trend to a new level by tying a scarf on your head, then braiding it right into a side braid. I love the illusion of really long hair this also achieves.

5 WAYS TO STYLE A LITTLE BLACK DRESS

Nothing beats the perfect little black dress. It hugs your body in just the right way, happens to go with every occasion, and remains as timeless as ever. While I love rocking my favorite LBD on its own, it also makes a great base layer for a number of different looks. This guide can also serve as a packing list for those who like to travel light.

LOOK 1

ADD A STATEMENT NECKLACE TO YOUR LBD:
This look is as simple as finding the right statement piece. I love necklaces with tons of color and texture (surprise, surprise), so choose one with tiered beads to create a fringed look.

LOOK 2

PAIR YOUR LBD WITH A BOLD BLAZER AND BOOTS:
This is basically the perfect day-to-night outfit. The blazer dresses things up for your workday and doubles as a layer for a brisk evening. The boots dress things down while still maintaining your refined style.

LOOK 3

LAYER A MAXI OVER YOUR LBD: Who says a floral print is just for the beach? Wear your LBD as a sleeveless top and layer a playful patterned skirt on the bottom for a fun and different look.

LOOK 4

FAKE A PENCIL SKIRT WITH A BELT AND BUTTON-DOWN: Never underestimate the power of a thick elastic belt: it'll instantly add shape to the most shapeless of outfits. In this case, it makes it easy to pretend that your dress is a skirt! Put on a button-down and "tuck it into" your belt, and no one will be the wiser.

LOOK 5

SHORTEN UP YOUR LBD: For a night out, shorten that dress right up! This definitely depends on the texture and fit of your little black dress. In this case, I was able to fold the bottom hem right underneath the dress to create a shortened effect. Secure with a safety pin or two if you think the hem will come undone. Pair with bold leggings or tights, and you're hot to trot.

MYPANTONE: This app is so "smart" it's creepy. Once you give it access, it will identify all the photos you've taken or sourced online, then match them to Pantone's collection of more than 13,000 colors. It can show you which colors you lean toward—whether for clothing or for home decor—so that you can make smarter decisions that are on-brand with your personality when you shop. It's basically the Shazam of color!

THIRDLOVE: Throw out your tape measure. This app uses scientific data to perfectly measure your bra size using nothing but a few photos of you from various angles.

POSE: Need advice on what to wear? Take a selfie, then send it to the Pose community to get instant feedback. It's like having all your girlfriends over . . . without having all your girlfriends over.

POSHMARK AND THREADFLIP: Before throwing your old clothes away, consider making some money on them instead. These two apps are like online consignment stores, letting you quickly upload images of clothes you no longer want, then collecting the cash once they sell.

RENT THE RUNWAY: If you've always wanted to wear a designer dress but don't have the money to buy one, why not rent one instead? Rent the Runway is my go-to for any formal affair.

LE TOTE: Often called the Netflix of fashion, Le Tote is a service that sends you multiple articles of clothing to wear, especially chosen for you by a stylist who has done his or her research on your style. Keep the clothes for as short or long a time as you want; once you return them, you'll be shipped a whole new set. This is my favorite way to keep a bit of variety in my wardrobe without having to shop all the time.

CUSTOM CLOTHING: All kinds of sites now exist that let you virtually create clothes tailored to your specifications. Want some custom heels or booties? Shop at Shoes of Prey. Or how about a unique, custom-designed dress? Bow & Drape will become your best friend. For running shoes, you really can't beat Nike ID. Even companies like Converse now let you customize their kicks. This is a mega-trend that will continue to grow and is here to stay.

FLORA: Care to turn your clothes into wearable electronics? Flora is an Arduino-powered microcontroller that can be sewn right into your clothing to enable amazing new fashions like light-up skirts, a location-aware jacket, or a scarf that can change colors.

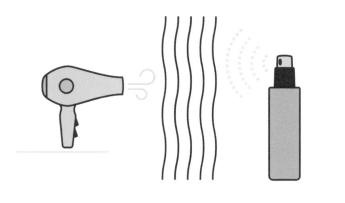

Spray with water, then dry with blow dryer.

Hang in bathroom during hot shower.

Give it a quick spin in the dryer.

Use a flat iron for collars and cuffs.

HACK: SMARTER WAYS TO PACK A SUITCASE

I'm all about traveling light and, in fact, pride myself on never taking more than a carry-on for trips that are 10 days or less. How do I do it? These handy traveling tips!

1. Instead of folding your clothes, roll 'em up! This is a more efficient use of space and still keeps your clothes relatively wrinkle-free.

2. Use shower caps as shoe bags. You don't want all the dirt on your shoes getting all over your clothes.

3. Pack belts and socks inside your shoes. This helps shoes keep their shape and means you can fit more stuff in that little suitcase!

4. If you're traveling with a curling iron or flat iron, bring a tea towel or pot holder to wrap it up. That way you don't have to wait for it to cool down to pack your suitcase.

This is a hack I've seen all over the web, and it's so spot-on that I use it in my own closet! Simply cut a pool noodle into quarters and place the noodle pieces in your boots to keep them stiff. It's as easy as that.

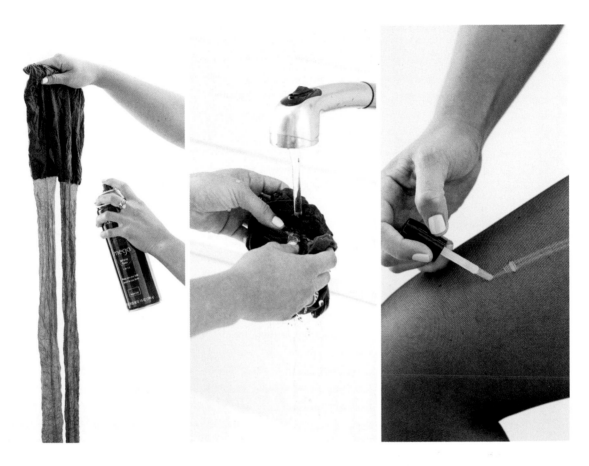

1. Spray tights with hair spray before you put them on.

2. Always wash tights by hand.

3. Use clear nail polish to fix runs as they happen.

DIY PROJECTS

JEWELRY ORGANIZER

MATERIALS	ASSORTED DRAWER KNOBS, PULLS, AND HANDLES
	SQUARE PIECE OF WOOD
	WHITE SPRAY PAINT
	NEON SPRAY PAINT (MATTE, NOT GLOSSY)

TOOLS	SANDPAPER
	DRILL
	MARKER

Can you guess where all the materials for this hip jewelry organizer came from? The hardware store! For real. I turned a bunch of drawer knobs, pulls, and handles into hooks for my favorite necklaces, bracelets, and earrings. Consider this part of Hardware Hacks 101—the hardware store really is one of my favorite places to go for creative inspiration.

STEP 1: First things first: you need a piece of wood to attach these knobs to. I had the folks at the hardware store cut this one to 24 inches by 24 inches. Make sure the wood is thick enough for the knobs to be screwed into it. Use sandpaper to smooth out any roughness.

STEP 2: Now it's time to paint all those knobs and drawer pulls. I chose a neon color palette. You will probably need two coats on each knob, sometimes three. As with all spray paint projects, you should do this outside or somewhere that is extremely well ventilated.

STEP 3: While the first coat of paint on the knobs is drying, use white spray paint to paint your wood white. You can also use regular house paint, but it will take way longer to dry.

STEP 4: Once everything is dry, head back to your worktable and lay out all the knobs on your board.

STEP 5: Use a marker to indicate where you need to drill holes to attach each piece.

STEP 6: Now drill all those holes!

STEP 7: Attach your knobs. It may help to have a friend hold up the board so you can access both sides.

STEP 8: Adorn with your favorite accessories!

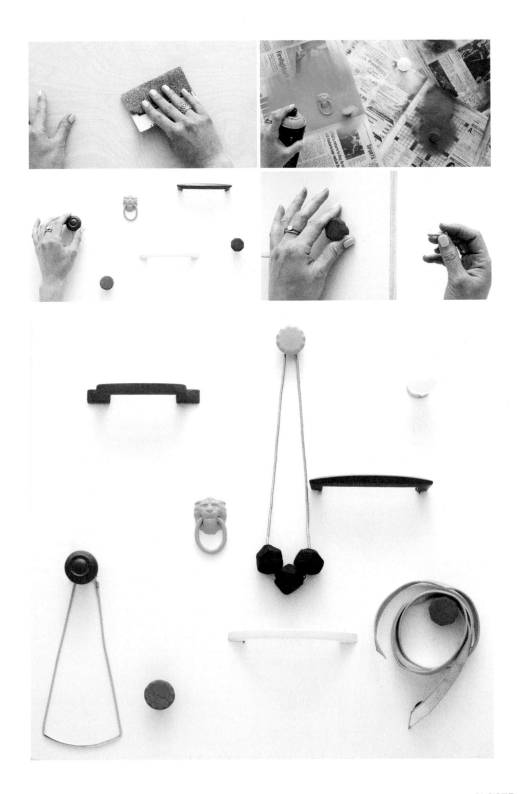

CLOSET PROJECTS
DIY MAXI SKIRT

MATERIALS	JERSEY FABRIC
	ELASTIC BAND
	MATCHING THREAD

TOOLS	SEWING MACHINE
	IRON
	MEASURING TAPE
	FABRIC SCISSORS

A comfy maxi skirt is a must-have for pretty much any woman, but did you know that it's super-easy to make your own? Like, *really* easy. Instead of buying a new one every time you need a refresh, you can simply whip out your sewing machine for a couple quick stitches. Don't blame me if you end up with a maxi skirt in every color under the sun! Okay fine, yes, blame me.

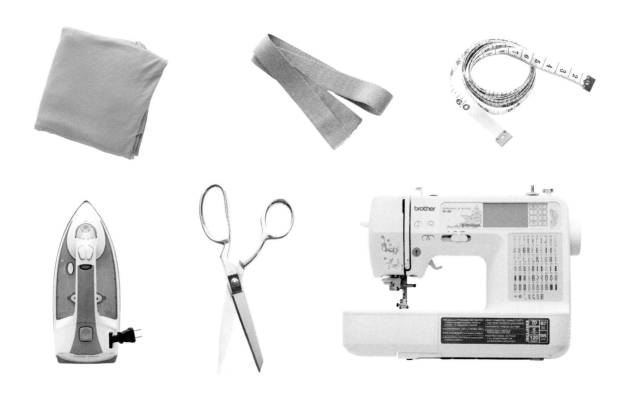

STEP 1: Fold your fabric in half.

STEP 2: Measure the waist of the skirt, adding an extra inch to each side to account for the seam. (You'll need to measure your own waist to determine the number of inches.)

STEP 3: Mark your measurements with pins.

STEP 4: Decide how long you want your skirt to be and then cut each side creating a gentle A-line. Pin your pieces of fabric together.

STEP 5: Sew along each side. Hem the waist of the skirt by folding over the edge twice and then sew, leaving a half-inch margin.

STEP 6: Fold the waist over and iron it to create a waistband.

STEP 7: Stitch around the waistband, leaving an opening wide enough to fit your elastic band.

STEP 8: Cut your elastic band about an inch smaller than your waist measurement, then add a safety pin to the end of the elastic and pull it through the waistband. The fabric will bunch up, but that's okay.

STEP 9: Sew both ends of the elastic together.

STEP 10: Sew the opening closed, and also sew through the elastic to keep it in place.

STEP 11: Hem the bottom of your skirt and trim any excess thread.

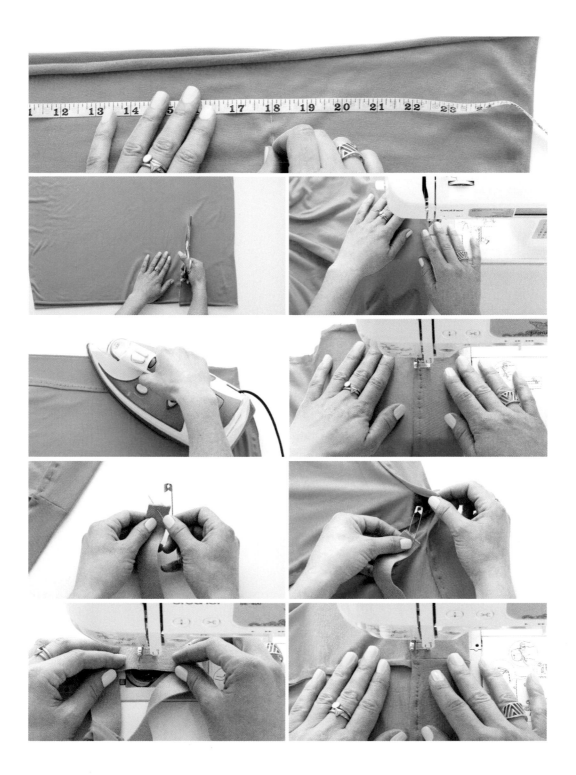

20-MINUTE SHOE RACK

MATERIALS	WOODEN BOARDS
	SCREWS
	WHITE ACRYLIC PAINT

TOOLS	WOOD GLUE
	DRILL
	MEASURING TAPE
	SANDPAPER
	SPONGE BRUSHES

Got a few too many shoes for the bottom of your closet or the entryway of your apartment? Do yourself a favor and whip up this easy-as-pie shoe rack. I promise it will take you less than 20 minutes!

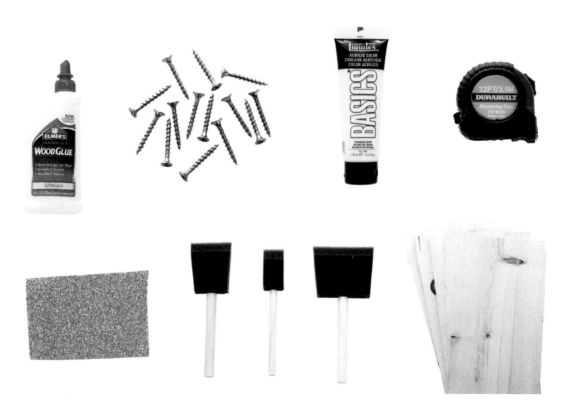

STEP 1: As with any wood project, the first thing to do is to sand your wood to smooth out any roughness.

STEP 2: Measure the halfway point on one slat of wood so you know where you want the middle shelf to go.

STEP 3: Measure two inches from the edge on both sides.

STEP 4: Squeeze a line of wood glue onto the edge of one of the slats you'll be using as a shelf.

STEP 5: Press the wood glue into the wood slat. Then drill in those screws. The glue will lock in with the screws, making your shelves secure.

STEP 6: Finally, add white edging to the whole piece with white acrylic paint. This will give the shelf a more refined and modern look.

NOTES

WOVEN CHAIN STATEMENT NECKLACE

MATERIALS	
	GOLD CHAIN
	GOLD JUMP RINGS
	CLASP
	EMBROIDERY FLOSS
	RHINESTONE CHAIN
	SILVER CHAIN

TOOLS	
	NEEDLE-NOSE PLIERS
	ROUND-NOSE PLIERS
	WIRE CUTTERS
	SCISSORS
	EMBROIDERY NEEDLE
	G-S HYPO CEMENT

I'm pretty much obsessed with statement necklaces, but they can be really expensive. So why not make your own? Here I'll show you how to turn basic chain and embroidery floss into a conversation-worthy piece.

STEP 1: Lay out all of your chain in a design you like. I went with a gold, silver, gold, silver, gold pattern. Cut the chain based on the measurement around your neck.

STEP 2: Use the needle to thread your first piece of embroidery floss through the first two lengths of chain.

STEP 3: Tie off the embroidery floss at the end.

STEP 4: Use a needle to weave through the two pieces of chain, connecting them with the embroidery floss.

STEP 5: Keep doing this, rotating colors for each section. Then bring your needle back through to secure the whole thing.

STEP 6: Tie off the embroidery floss at one end.

STEP 7: Use G-S Hypo cement (or any jewelry glue) to glue down the end of the embroidery floss. This ensures that your necklace doesn't unravel.

STEP 8: Cut an additional piece of gold chain and attach to one end of your necklace with a jump ring. Then attach another jump ring to the end of that.

STEP 9: Finally, use a jump ring to attach your clasp to the other end.

MIXED MATERIAL BRACELET

While I love the mixed material trend, it can often look too crafty, like a bead store that exploded. The key to creating a bracelet that has lots of different textures and materials is to stick to a consistent color palette so that everything blends together beautifully.

MATERIALS	VARIETY OF BEADS
	EMBROIDERY FLOSS
	CHAIN
	CORD ENDS
	MULTI-LOOP ENDS
	JUMP RINGS
	CLASP
	MONOFILAMENT
	RHINESTONE CHAIN

TOOLS	NEEDLE-NOSE PLIERS
	E6000 GLUE
	G-S HYPO CEMENT
	EMBROIDERY NEEDLE

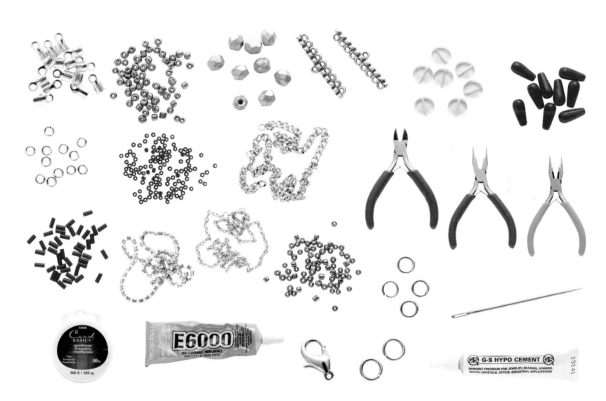

STEP 1: Measure your wrist and cut monofilament accordingly. Attach a cord end to the first string of monofilament, then string beads on.

STEP 2: Squeeze a little E6000 glue into a cord end, then clamp it onto the end of your first strand.

STEP 3: Cut a length of rhinestones and add cord ends to each end. Braid your embroidery floss, weave string into chain (as with the statement necklace I made on page 281), and string a few more strands of beads.

STEP 4: Lay out all of your strands. This is the time to make any necessary length adjustment—but hopefully you won't have to.

STEP 5: Use needle-nose pliers to attach jump rings to your multi-loop end.

STEP 6: Once you've done that with every strand, attach a jump ring onto one end.

STEP 7: Finally, attach your clasp!

How awesome do all of those materials look together?

THE FUTURE CLOSET

3D CLOTHING PRINTER: If you think
3D printers that can print plastic are cool,
just wait till you see one that can print
fabric. Many technologists already have
prototypes of machines that can weave
fabrics together right in front of your
eyes. And their goal is to let you recycle
your worn clothing back into the machine

to break apart the fibers and print something completely new. Imagine
the possibilities for cost savings and eco-friendliness. Additionally, as 3D
printers have become more advanced, fashion designers have begun to
dream about selling customizable versions of their designs online. What
if you break a heel? Just print another!

BODY SCANNING: If the thought of printing
out your own clothes on demand isn't exciting
enough, what if I told you that every single piece
of clothing you may own—including your shoes—
will fit you like a glove? When body scanning
technology becomes more readily available, it
will let you take a full 360-degree scan of your
body, feet and all. Then, using your precise

measurements, you can print clothes on demand that fit perfectly. Will
this finally spell the end of tailoring? Imagine the possibilities for bras,
shoes, and more.

DIGITAL CLOSET: If you have ever seen the movie *Clueless,* then I know you have had more than one fantasy about being able to browse your entire closet from your computer. This reality isn't too far away. Several technology companies are working on ways to automatically take inventory of what you have in your closet, making it a more seamless process to get ready in the morning, pack for long vacations, mix and match outfits, and more.

CUSTOM CLOTHES: While many retailers are beginning to offer clothing customization, the fact that we are building a long-tail of self-manufacturing will enable us all to personalize our garments in new ways. When ordering clothes online in the future, not only will you be able to upload your personal body measurements to ensure the fit is perfect, but you'll also be able to customize colors, patterns, shapes, and more.

FASHION DESIGN 2.0: If you've ever watched a season of *Project Runway*, you know that in today's world, it's challenging to become a notable fashion designer. Once you get people to start recognizing you, you still need to get your sketches and designs into the hands of major retail buyers in order to get your products carried in their stores.

But in tomorrow's world, that will all change. If people are able to print and make their own clothes on demand, the retailer you buy from matters much less. Indie designers will be able to reach millions of consumers by simply uploading their designs to the web. So all of you fashion designer hopefuls, start practicing your sketches!

SMART GLASSES: Even if you've never had an issue with your eyes, you may still find yourself wearing glasses in the future . . . or at least contacts. Google is leading the charge in creating a new type of wearable technology called Google Glass, which essentially lets you wear glasses that act as computer screens: these glasses can browse the web, record video and photos, and even react to the sound of your voice or the direction of your gaze. While they look a little silly now, this technology will soon be embedded into fashionworthy glasses, sunglasses, and contacts and will enable you to become much more informed about the world around you as you are living in it. I for one am excited about the day when I can follow a recipe without using my hands to turn the pages or screens of a cookbook—the directions will be right in front of me, through my specs.

NOTES

BATHROOM

Gone are the days when women were practically forced to wear rollers in their hair and lipstick on their pouts. In today's world, women are choosing beauty routines that are the easiest and most comfortable for them, ranging from totally bare to completely made-up.

I personally enjoy getting made up (except on weekends and beach vacations—those are perfect times to go au naturel), but I don't always have the time. I've usually got about 15 to 20 minutes *tops* to get both my hair and my makeup done in the morning—and that's starting with wet hair. (PS: Isn't blow-drying the worst, most time-sucking thing ever? When will someone invent a new solution for that?) Naturally, I've had to find a routine that works.

Whatever your beauty preference, there are many ways to make yourself just as bright, bold, and beautiful as the pros would make you at the salon or makeup counter . . . no stylists needed. In fact, when I started this career, I used to pay a stylist to do my hair and makeup anytime I had to do a photo or video shoot—which was quite often! Now, though, I've been taught the secrets, and I feel confident enough in my DIY beauty skills to not need a pro at my side any longer. And because my mother always told me to pay it forward, it's time to pass those tricks on to you.

BEAUTY BASICS

When it comes to beauty, I'm all about keeping things simple. Though there are days that I rock nothing but a touch of lip gloss, these are the 12 essentials every gal should have in their makeup kit.

MOISTURIZER: Every makeup look should start with your favorite moisturizer to hydrate your skin and protect your face from harsh elements.

FOUNDATION: Make sure to buy a color that matches your skin pigment perfectly. No one likes splotchy foundation lines! And if you tend to tan easily, try buying two shades—one for summer and the other for winter. You can blend the two when you're in between colors in spring and fall. Your skin will look silky smooth if you do it right.

CONCEALER: Your concealer should match your foundation perfectly, or you can go a shade lighter for a brightening effect depending on where you'll be using it.

SETTING POWDER: A lot of people skip setting powder, but I swear by it. Using a fluffy powder brush, apply a translucent powder by "stippling." Stippling means pressing the brush onto your face lightly, without dragging along the skin so you don't smear or rub off your base.

BRONZER: Bronzer is not just about faking that beginning-of-summer glow. It can also be used for contouring. I recommend using a golden bronzer with a slight shimmer to get that naturally sun-kissed finish. When using, be sure to blend into your ears and down onto your neck as well to avoid any harsh lines.

BLUSH: The one thing most women don't know about blush is how multi-purpose it is. Not only can it add some rosy color to your cheeks, but you can also use it to contour your face—it's like instant Photoshop.

HIGHLIGHTER: The right highlighter is just what you need to amp up your natural glow! Using a flat foundation brush, apply a small amount of shimmering highlighter along the natural line of your cheekbones under where you brushed your blush on your cheeks. Blend the highlighter up into the blush to get that luminous youthful sheen in a snap!

EYESHADOW: Eyeshadow is a blessing and a curse. There are so many ways to use it, but if you feel inadequate at your skills, you can end up with a big ol' mess on those pretty little eyes. Keep it simple by using a palette of three shades: neutral, dark, and light.

EYELINER: Perhaps my favorite tool in the makeup stack, eyeliner is clutch for making your eyes look way bigger than they actually are. As with eyeshadow, there are many ways you can use a liner (cat eyes, wings, etc.), but my basic routine is to use a darker liner for the top lid and a softer liner for the bottom. I find it tends to add much more dimension while keeping my eyes looking big and brown.

EYELASH CURLER: For maximum length and eyelash volume, use an eyelash curler before moving on to mascara.

MASCARA: Mascara is my daily coffee in makeup form. It seriously tends to wake me up! A few strokes, and my eyes are much wider open. Be careful going too bold with mascara for daytime looks. The "Twiggy" look is best suited for evening dinners and dance parties.

LIPS: Whether you go for lip gloss or lipstick, I consider lip liner a daily essential for adding more dimension to my pout. I love to wear a deep red statement lipstick for special occasions, and a softer pink on the daily.

THE 10-MINUTE FACE

Every woman should have a go-to makeup routine that can be done in under ten minutes. When I am pressed for time, these are the products and methods I use to perk up my face in a flash. To cut even more time, try skipping out on eyeshadow and liner, but continue to use mascara to make those beautiful eyes pop.

MOISTURIZER AND FOUNDATION: Start off by moisturizing your face—this will not only hydrate the skin, but will also protect from harsh elements. When you're applying foundation, always be sure to use downstrokes on your face as this is the best way to cover pores and fine hairs.

CONCEALER: Apply a small amount with a concealer brush, then use your finger to gently blend into your skin. I recommend using your finger for this because the heat helps spread the concealer more evenly, especially when dealing with more delicate areas like under your eyes.

BRONZER AND BLUSH: Use bronzer to contour your face by making an "E" stroke on each side, moving up to your forehead and down to your jawline. When applying blush, smile and sweep a small amount of blush from the apple of your cheek up towards your temple, avoiding the area directly under your eyes. Then brush outwards lightly towards your hairline.

EYE SHADOW AND LINER: Go for neutral, dark, and light shadow. Spread the neutral all over the lid, blend in a dark shadow line at the crease, and highlight underneath your brows and in between your eye ducts with the light shadow. For liner, I recommend using a darker liner for the top lid and a softer one for the bottom.

MASCARA: And now, it's time for that finishing touch. Before applying mascara, use an eyelash curler to curl your lashes. Then, mascara time. I always give the top lashes a few waves of the wand and only stroke the bottom for the days when I'm dressing up.

LIP: My go-to lip is just a touch of gloss, but if you do like to use lipstick, be sure you are either lining your lips beforehand or that your hands are steady enough to stay inside your lip lines. Give a Kleenex a quick blot and you're ready to roll!

HOW TO MAKE YOUR EYES LOOK BIGGER

When it comes to making your eyes look bigger, look no further than the classic cat eye. Ladies have been rocking winged liner for decades now, and for good reason!

STEP 1 To create a smoky effect, use dark black shadow to add more dimension to the outer corners of your eyes.

STEP 2 Extend liner along your upper lash line, drawing it beyond the outer corners of your eyes into a cat-eye shape.

STEP 3 To make your eyes really pop, apply a white or nude liner inside your bottom lashes along your lower lash line.

STEP 4 Finish off with mascara. Meow!

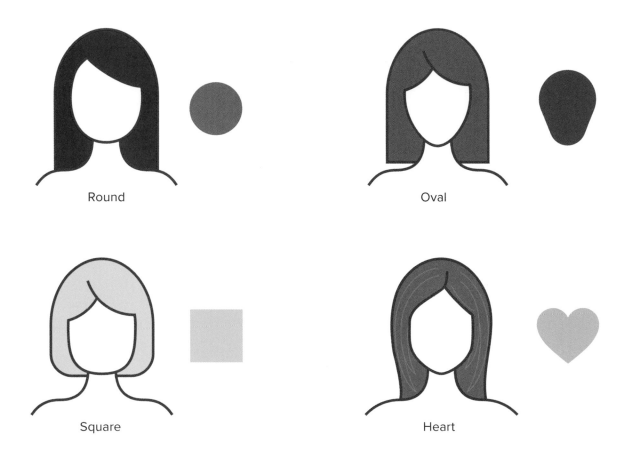

Round

Oval

Square

Heart

Why is face shape important? Answer: different hairstyles look better (or worse) on different faces. For instance, if you have a heart-shaped face (like myself), you can make your pointy chin a little less severe with face-framing layers. I also often curl my hair outward (away from my face) to add width to my jawline and thus balance to my overall face.

THE SKINNY ON SPF

You've probably heard this one a million times, but it goes without saying that SPF is a *must* to apply on a daily basis. Be sure to slather some on your face and neck (and heck, why not even cover those pretty arms and legs?) before putting your makeup on. And be sure that your SPF is at least 30+ for the best UV coverage. Trust me, you'll thank me when you're 50 and have way fewer wrinkles and sun spots than all of your girlfriends.

SUBSTITUTES FOR BEAUTY PRODUCTS

Whether you are short on cash, can't get to the store, or simply prefer to use more natural products on your skin, try substituting these products for your standard beauty products and see just how well they compete.

OATMEAL

Oats have been used in skin care since around 2000 BC, and their use has even received recognition from the Food and Drug Administration. Oatmeal has antioxidant and anti-inflammatory properties that help treat sensitive skin. Try pouring a cup of oats into your next warm bath, mixing oats with water and honey to create a soothing face mask, or blending oats with coconut oil and brown sugar to create a 100% natural exfoliating cleanser.

MAYONNAISE

Surprisingly enough, mayonnaise is a fantastic moisturizer. Many substitute it for their hair conditioner (make sure to shampoo AFTER you use it), use it as a cooling face mask, and even apply it to their nails to soften cuticles.

OLIVE OIL

Olive oil, like mayonnaise, is fantastic at moisturizing your skin. Use a dab on your face before bed at night to keep your skin looking bright and fabulous, smack some on chapped lips, or try integrating it into your hair routine by mixing olive oil with warm water and leaving it on your wet locks for at least five to ten minutes before shampooing. It's a hot oil treatment for a fraction of the cost!

PREPARATION H

As gross as this product may seem, it's actually phenomenal at de-puffing those pesky bags under your tired eyes. Dab a bit on before putting on your makeup and see the amazing transformation.

AVOCADO

Not only can avocado help moisturize the skin in ways similar to the effect of mayonnaise or olive oil, but it also contains ingredients that can eliminate redness. To deal with blotchy skin, I often mash up a bit of avocado, blend it with whole yogurt and honey, then apply to my skin for about 15 minutes before washing it off. Try it for yourself to see if avocado works for you.

5-MINUTE BEACH WAVES

This look is seemingly effortless and a lot of fun to improvise. It's best described as a little bit of this and a little bit of that. You've got tousled waves, smooth curls, and beachy volume all packed into one look.

STEP 1 Use your curling iron as a curling wand and simply wrap small sections of hair around the curling iron, keeping the clip portion closed. Vary the sections you choose, from a half inch thick to two inches thick. Don't curl your entire head of hair—just sections here and there.

STEP 2 Then use the curling iron with the clip and add more curls to the mix. Again, you want to vary the thickness of the curl as well as where you place it. After you've added as many waves and curls as you like, scrunch your hair to make sure it flows together.

THREE WAYS TO ROCK A BRAID

Enter the braid. As classic as it is, the braid is always being reinvented and revived, and all modern gals should know a thing or two about how to mix up their own twisted locks. Here are my three go-to braided hairstyles.

CROWN HEADBAND

STEP 1 Lift the hair up on one side of your head and pin it away. Then pick up a section around a half-inch thick. Braid all the way to the end and secure with a small elastic.

STEP 2 Repeat the same steps on the other side of your head.

STEP 3 To add volume to the front, back comb the top center of your hair. Pull this part of the hair back—it will serve to add volume to the front of the hair when your braids come together to form a headband.

STEP 4 Bring each braid up and over the top of your head, securing it with bobby pins on the opposite side.

FISHTAIL SIDE BRAID

STEP 1 Make a heavy side part. Bring hair over to the heavier side of the part and split your locks into two sections. Pick up a small piece of hair from the outside of one section and cross it over, into the other section.

STEP 2 Repeat this process on each side until you have around 3" of hair left from your ends, then secure with an elastic.

STEP 3 Gently pull each side of the braid apart to loosen up the style. (Notice that the distance from the bottom is now smaller than 3".)

STEP 4 Pin back some of the loose hairs that may have fallen out of the braid to finalize the look.

WATERFALL BRAID

STEP 1 Start with a small section on one side of your head. Split this section into three parts. Begin by braiding a normal French braid with these three sections.

STEP 2 Once the section of hair that is against your head is braided, drop one of the pieces down so that it flows into the rest of your hair.

STEP 3 Pick up the next section of hair and braid it into this braid—again dropping a piece that is closest to your head.

STEP 4 Repeat until you've covered the whole side of your head. Then cue up "Waterfalls" by TLC.

NAIL ART BASICS

There are some seriously talented nail artists out there, but I'm here to show you a handful of super simple tricks that any amateur nail polish enthusiast can master.

POLKA DOTS: Start by painting a base coat in a color of your choice. I went with gold. Let your nails dry. Then pour a drop of nail polish onto a paper plate or dish. Dip a bobby pin in it, then polka-dot away!

HALF MOON: For this look, you can use three-hole reinforcement stickers, or the circle-shaped stickers found in the stationery section of any grocery store or pharmacy. Start with a red base coat. Let it dry all the way—longer than you might think. Cut stickers in half and place them on your dry painted nails. Then paint over them with purple polish. Let nails dry again, peel off the stickers, and you're done!

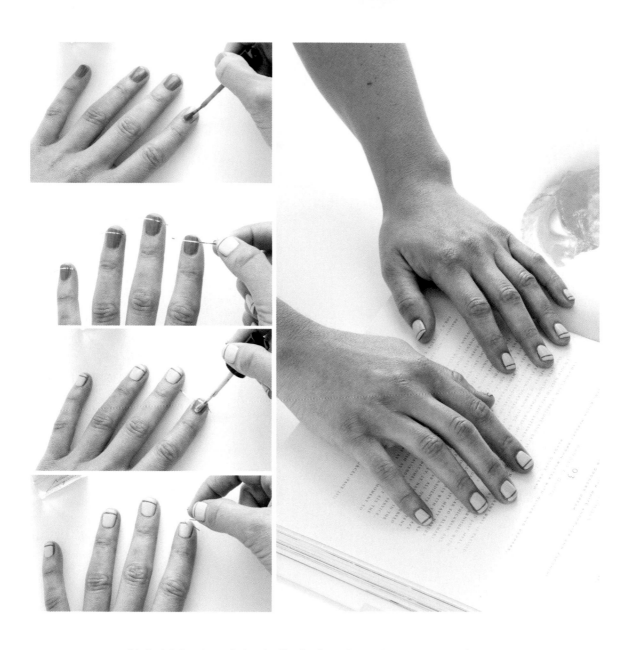

STRIPES: Nail striping tape is basically the best invention ever . . . at least in the world of nail art. It's like any kind of tape—just way, way, way skinnier! For a simple stripe on all of your nails, start with a base coat as usual. Let it dry, then place strips of nail tape on each of your nails. Paint with your second color, let your nails dry again, and peel off the tape.

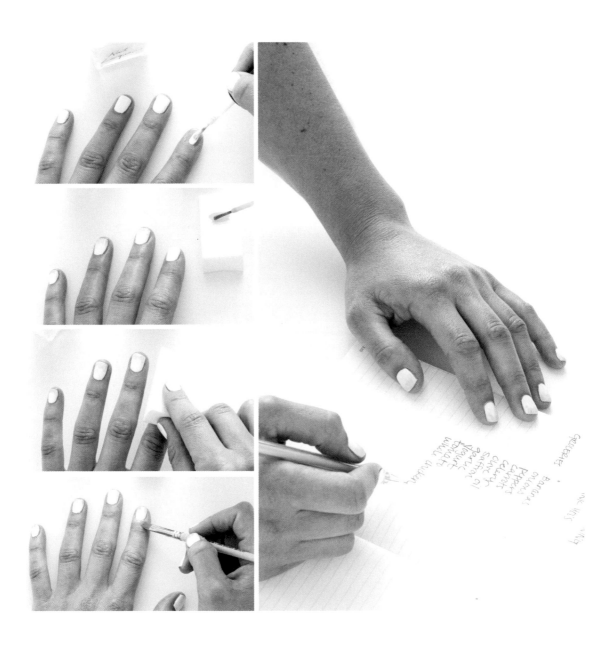

OMBRE: Finally, to create the ombre look, I'll show you how to use a makeup sponge. Start with a white base coat. Then paint onto a makeup sponge in a way that matches the shape of your nail. Start with thick polish at the bottom and fade upward. Then press it onto your nail! Use nail polish remover to clean up any excess polish.

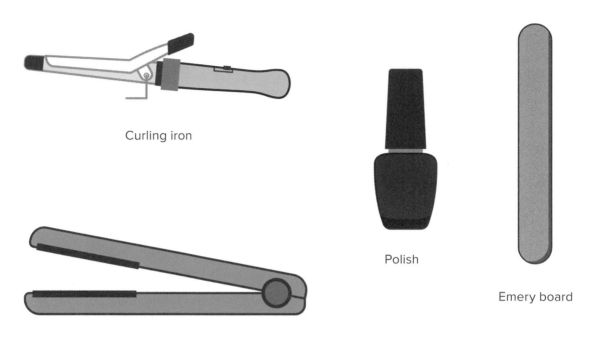

Curling iron

Polish

Emery board

Straightening iron

Wide-tooth comb

Foundation and powder

Eyeliner

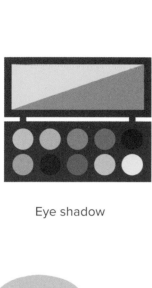

Eye shadow

Lip gloss

Mascara

Blush

Anti-aging oil

Cleanser

SPF

Lotion

NAILSNAPS: Use any image or design to create stickable nail art. Perfect for Instagram lovers!

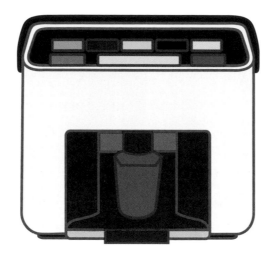

PALETTE: This is GENIUS. Create nail polish colors using your smartphone. Take a photo of any random color, scan your phone, and the Palette will make the polish for you instantly. Soon it may even be able to apply it directly to your nails, just like a manicurist would. Bye-bye, nail salons?

INSTYLE HAIRSTYLE TRY ON: Perfect for finding the right hairstyle for your face, this app also lets you try on famous celebrity 'dos before you tell your stylist to chop. I, for one, enjoy trying on Jen Aniston's classic cut from time to time.

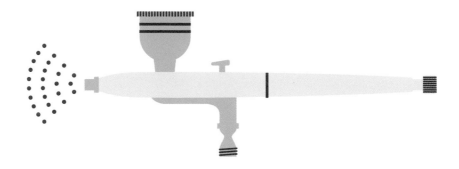

AIRBRUSH: Hands down the best way to get a flawless-looking complexion. An airbrush is more time-intensive than regular foundation, but will create a stunning effect on your skin. I recommend using one for all formal events and special occasions.

SPF BRACELET/APP: Goodbye skin cancer? Now there's tech that will tell you when to reapply your SPF. New bracelets and apps will prompt you with alerts to slather on more lotion as the day goes on.

STYLESEAT: If you hate having to search Yelp or Google for a stylist, call to make an appointment, then drive to the salon, look no further than StyleSeat, a service that lets you browse hair and nail stylists who come directly to *you!*

PLUM PERFECT: Snap a selfie and this app will instantly analyze your skin tone and hair color, then suggest products and shades that will look best on you.

AN ALL-NATURAL FACE MASK FOR ALL FOUR SEASONS

Are you ready for this? Your favorite breakfast indulgence might also be your new go-to DIY face mask. The only ingredients you need are Greek yogurt and honey! Start with those two basics and add in any mix of additional ingredients, depending on the season, and you'll be sure to always put your best face forward. The lactic acid in Greek yogurt (full fat) is a gentle exfoliator that will help clean out your pores. Plus, the combination of fat from the milk in the yogurt and the honey, which is a natural humectant, moisturizes and nourishes your skin.

To make the yogurt and honey base, combine two tablespoons of Greek yogurt with one teaspoon of honey. Then add more ingredients based on the season, your skin type, and what your skin currently needs. Read on for my recommendations by season. With any of these, it's best to consult a dermatologist or aesthetician to make sure you don't have an allergic reaction to the ingredients before using them.

SPRING

Lemon juice (one lemon wedge): Lemons are a super-fruit in pretty much any category. When it comes to your face, lemons are your go-to for banishing oily skin and evening out dark spots, acne scars, and wrinkles because they act as natural toners and cleansers.

Lavender buds (half a tablespoon) plus essential oil (two drops): Famous for being one of the most calming scents around, lavender is a good thing to keep on hand all year round. Mix a bit of lavender oil into your honey and yogurt mix, and then keep the buds on your face to act as a natural exfoliator.

SUMMER

Fresh berries (equivalent of two to three strawberries): Berries are my key to making a delicious smoothie, and strawberries brighten your skin tone and happen to be packed with vitamin C, which will make your face very happy. Blueberries are amazingly natural antioxidants that help reduce lines and wrinkles. Or go for blackberries, which help fight acne and also act as a toner that polishes skin beautifully.

Orange juice (half a tablespoon) plus oatmeal (one tablespoon): This combo is a veritable one-two punch when it comes to firming up your skin. Oatmeal acts as a natural cleanser and moisturizes deeply to relieve dryness. Add orange juice to the mix and you've also got vitamin C and potassium, which help to tighten the skin, unclog pores, and fight blemishes.

FALL

Cinnamon (half a tablespoon): Cinnamon not only smells delicious but helps to dry out acne. It can also open up pores that need a little extra breathing room.

Pumpkin puree (one-quarter of a can) plus brown sugar (one tablespoon): Doesn't the combo of pumpkin puree and brown sugar sound like a pie that's just waiting to be baked? But seriously, pumpkin is packed with tons of vitamins and restorative powers that can help reverse skin damage. And if you're familiar with sugar scrubs, you may already know that brown sugar is an excellent natural exfoliant.

WINTER

Kiwi (one whole kiwi peeled and mashed): Kiwi is a great add-in to help brighten your complexion. Plus, the seeds act as a mild exfoliant.

Avocado (half an avocado) plus egg whites (one egg white): Avocados are soothing to the skin, come packed with moisture, and have anti-inflammatory properties. Egg whites help shrink pores and promote strong, wrinkle-free skin. Combine the two to give wintry skin a blast of rejuvenation.

LEATHER MAKEUP BRUSH ORGANIZER

MATERIALS	LEATHER
	LEATHER CORD
	HEAT & BOND ULTRAHOLD, CUT TO 11 INCHES LONG AND 7 INCHES WIDE
	WIDE AND THIN POPSICLE STICKS

TOOLS	X-ACTO KNIFE
	CUTTING MAT
	SCISSORS (TO CUT HEAT & BOND— DO NOT USE FABRIC SCISSORS)
	FABRIC SCISSORS
	MEASURING TAPE
	IRON
	PEN

Now that you know how to use all the brushes in your makeup kit, how about organizing them for on-the-go beauty? In this project, I'll show you how to make a chic brush caddy out of gorgeous red leather. The key here is using a super-thin piece of leather, pleather, or vinyl so that it rolls up easily. This pouch holds six makeup brushes that are all about six inches long by half an inch wide.

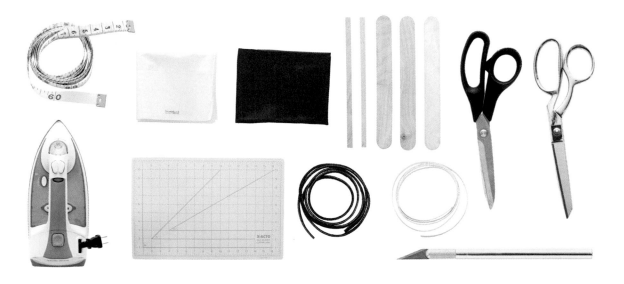

STEP 1: Cut your leather into a panel that's twenty-two inches long and seven inches wide. I measured this one based on my makeup brushes, which are six inches long by half an inch wide. You want about a half-inch of leather at the top and bottom of your brushes and about an inch on either end. You can adjust these measurements if your brushes are much larger or smaller than the ones I used.

STEP 2: On the back side of the leather, mark the panel in half. Then, mark the center line across the width of one side.

STEP 3: Mark a quarter-inch on either side of the center line. These are the guide lines you'll follow to make your cuts for your brushes.

STEP 4: Starting at about one inch away from the end, make two parallel incisions along the guide lines to create your brush loops for each makeup brush. The length will vary depending on the width of your brushes, between half an inch for thinner brushes and one and a half inches for wide brushes. Be sure to leave about half an inch of space in between each brush loop.

STEP 5: These loops need to be bigger than you think to actually hold the brushes. Be sure to test out the loops to see if they need to be bigger before moving on to the next step.

STEP 6: Cut Heat & Bond to eleven inches long and seven inches wide, add it to the back side of the intact part of your brush holder, and iron on according to the instructions.

STEP 7: Once that side has completely adhered, remove the paper and reserve and flip the brush loop side on top of it—it should be folded neatly in half.

STEP 8: Cut popsicle sticks into small rectangles and insert them into brush loops to prevent them from adhering to the Heat & Bond.

STEP 9: Lay the removed paper over the entire pouch and iron together according to the instructions. Once it has completely adhered, remove the popsicle sticks!

STEP 10: It's finally time to add the leather ties. Use your X-Acto knife to cut a small slit at the end of the roll.

STEP 11: String the ties through and tie a knot to secure.

That's a wrap!

THE FUTURE BATHROOM

FUTURE TOOTHBRUSH: Technologists are currently working on Bluetooth, light-enabled toothbrushes that can not only keep data on how long you are brushing but use light technology on the bristles to break down extra plaque and bacteria and also whiten teeth. I'm in!

MAKEUP CUSTOMIZATION: There are new devices in development— including Mink, a 3D printer for makeup—that will let you mix your own makeup on demand. Imagine a foundation that *finally* matches your skin tone perfectly, or being able to mix up a new palette of colored eye shadow on the fly. All of this will soon be a possibility.

WRINKLE-FIGHTING WIPES:

If you thought your makeup-removing wipes were cool, get excited! Because soon they will also contain ingredients that can smooth crow's-feet. And if you want

to take it a step further, some scientists say that we will soon also be able to use at-home hyaluronic acid gel patches to create the same wrinkle-filling injections that products like Botox currently offer. Just remember that wrinkles or no wrinkles, you should always appreciate your natural beauty.

HOME LASER HAIR REMOVAL:

Though there are already some products on the market, this is a tool that is becoming more and more refined for letting men and women DIY the removal of unwanted hair, wrinkles, sun spots, stretch marks, and potentially even tattoos. I've personally used laser hair removal treatments in the past and can

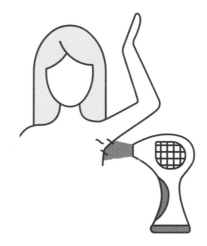

honestly say they are some of the best investments I've ever made. I save so much time and effort by no longer having to shave!

GRAY HAIR PILL: While some of us have no issues with turning gray over time, others will be excited to hear that scientists are working on a pill that may prevent hair from changing color. "The leukemia drug Gleevec causes some people to restore hair color. It's a matter of flipping the right gene switches in the DNA, turning the right expression up or down, like the volume control on a stereo. And women might have an even better way to color their hair at home: a heat-sensitive dye that would be activated by a hair-dryer or flatiron," speculates Brian M. Kinney, clinical assistant professor of plastic surgery at the University of Southern California in Los Angeles.

SMART MIRRORS: Even our mirrors are getting smarter. Your future bathroom mirror will soon be web-enabled to give you information like the daily news and weather while you get ready for the day. When you quickly glance in the mirror, it could tell you what type of products to 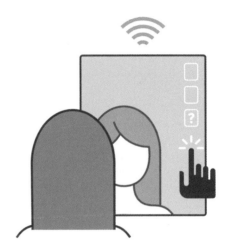 use on your skin that day. "A sensor that looks similar to a digital thermometer could be tethered to the mirror and connected to a built-in meter," says cosmetic dermatologist Dr. Daniel McDaniel. "You can pull out the sensor and touch it to the skin, measuring moisture, oiliness, and redness. If the meter says the skin is getting drier, you increase your moisturizer." And eventually mirrors may track your appearance over time, as well as allow you to see how your features could be changed with plastic surgery, or so says Andrew Dent, vice president of materials research at the Material ConneXion in New York City.

SUNSCREEN PILLS: Perhaps one of my favorites on this list (I hate slathering on sunscreen—it takes forever and I always miss a spot!), new pills are being developed that will protect your skin from the sun. Take them each morning with your coffee to ensure you are protected all day every day.

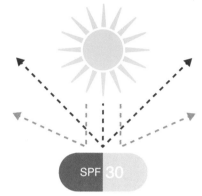

WORKSPACE

Even if you don't have a designated office, hobby, or craft room, I'm willing to bet there are places in your home where you feel most creative or productive. And if you're like 9.5% of the country, you might even call this space your official workplace.

The Internet has made it so that more of us can do our jobs from the comfort of our homes, a work style that has been more possible and socially acceptable for a decade or two now. Stay-at-home moms can also be CEOs. It's fantastic and truly astounding to see how many people are now making a living from inside the place where they do most of their living. This trend will only continue to expand. That's why it's important that our home workspace be a place where we can be most creative and efficient. Ideas are endless here! Similar to the closet, tools and supplies should be on display at all times so that you can strike up inspiration for a new project on a dime. Use your walls for notes, brainstorms, and big ideas. And make sure you have the technology essentials for getting the job done well and on time.

4 FOOLPROOF WAYS TO KEEP YOUR CREATIVE ROOM ORGANIZED

If you're an avid DIYer, you've probably fallen prey to bins, baskets, and boxes filled with tons of craft supplies, but you have no idea where anything is. I know that's happened to me and the whole crew here at Brit + Co time and time again. But with a few simple tricks, it's easy to keep your creative space just as organized as your Google Docs. Here are some of my favorite tools and tricks for organization.

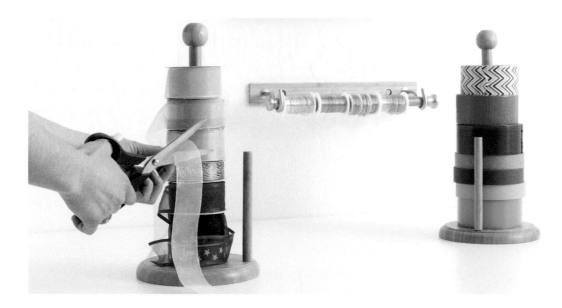

PAPER TOWEL HOLDERS: Who says paper towel holders are just for the kitchen? You can also use them to organize spools of ribbon, rolls of tape, and wire. Plus, a paper towel holder makes it easy to cut off whatever length you need without messing up your beautiful organization.

 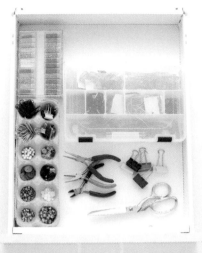 

ICE CUBE TRAYS AND EGG CARTONS: Got a thing for paper clips, sequins, or buttons? Then you probably need a way to organize them. Ice cube trays and egg cartons (painted a bright color, of course) make great caddies for all those itty-bitty odds and ends.

PLASTIC TRAYS: Never underestimate how much a basic plastic tray will help keep your drawers or desktop organized. These are great for storing sharp things like scissors and utility knives that you don't want rolling around loose. They're also good for storing paint and glue so that you don't end up with unwanted spills.

MINI CHEST OF DRAWERS: I took a cue from the bead store for this hack. If you work with lots of beads, studs, hex nuts, and other small notions, a chest of drawers such as this will be your best friend. Put everything in its own drawer, and label each drawer by gluing the thing that's in it on the front of the drawer to serve as the handle or knob.

Everything
you can
Imagine
is real

- PABLO PICASSO

THE ART OF THE CHALKBOARD WALL

Chalkboard paint has quickly become an essential for DIYers. Though I love using it in unusual ways for things like jar labels and gift tags, nothing beats a chalkboard wall. It's a great conversation piece and on-the-wall guestbook for your home or office, and it's especially awesome for impromptu brainstorming. Yes, I still brainstorm in analog sometimes!

TO SEW OR NOT TO SEW

While my mother's and grandmothers' generations were brought up knowing how to sew, most of my peers have no clue how to do anything but a basic stitch. And yes, while sewing is a great skill to have, there are several ways to create beautiful things using fabric glue or other materials that do not require a sewing machine. So don't freak out if you still don't know the basics of Sewing 101—it shouldn't deter you from being a DIY superstar.

Brit Tip:
When you're cutting paper or any other material, get a smoother line by turning the material, not the scissors. You'd be surprised at how much easier it is to cut using this technique!

THE LOWDOWN ON GLUES

Gone are the days when Elmer's was the only glue you used. Now that you're all grown up, you should know about all the different types of glues and what they're used for.

CRAFT GLUE: for use with plastic, paper, fabric, or Styrofoam

E6000 (BY FAR MY FAVORITE GLUE!): for use with metal, wood, fabric, rubber, paper, plastic, glass, concrete, or Styrofoam

SUPERGLUE: for use with plastic, ceramics, glass, or metal

HOT GLUE: for use with plastic, paper, ceramics, wood, glass, fabric, or Styrofoam

MOD PODGE: or DIY your own with cornstarch and water

SPRAY ADHESIVE: for use with plastic, paper, fabric, or Styrofoam

FABRIC GLUE: for use with paper or fabric

RUBBER CEMENT: for use with paper, wood, fabric, or Styrofoam

NOTES

BASIC PRODUCTS YOU NEED

These are the basic supplies that all amateur makers should have. This list is by no means complete, but it includes what I use most often when I'm creating.

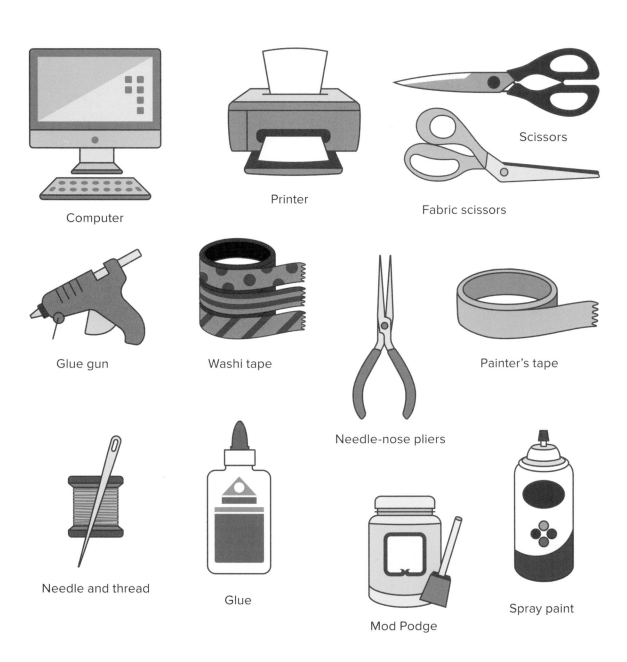

Computer

Printer

Scissors

Fabric scissors

Glue gun

Washi tape

Needle-nose pliers

Painter's tape

Needle and thread

Glue

Mod Podge

Spray paint

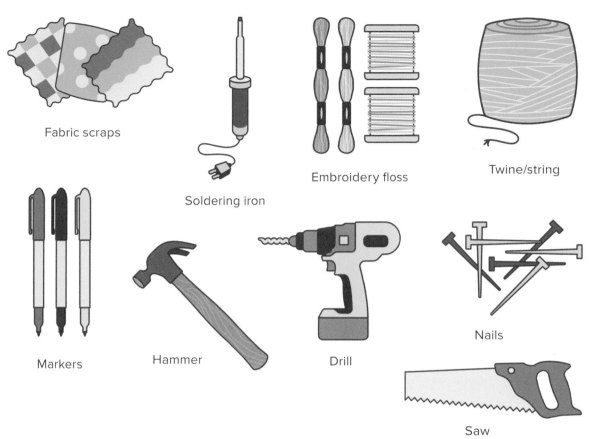

Fabric scraps

Soldering iron

Embroidery floss

Twine/string

Markers

Hammer

Drill

Nails

Saw

TOOLS THAT ARE NICE TO HAVE

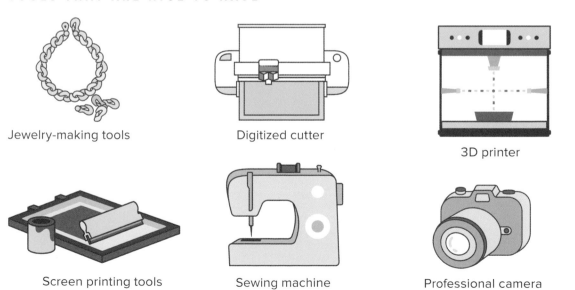

Jewelry-making tools

Digitized cutter

3D printer

Screen printing tools

Sewing machine

Professional camera

APPS

IFONTMAKER: This app turns your handwriting into a digital font. Great to use for custom stationery, text overlays on digital photos, "handwritten" thank-you notes, and more!

iLEVEL: Make sure all of your drawings and objects are straight with the iLevel. You may never buy a real level again.

MURAL.LY: Basically, it's Google Docs meets Pinterest meets Post-its meets everything wonderful in the universe.

PAPER: An amazing digital sketchbook that is as close to a real sketchbook as anything I've ever seen. It's my favorite for big brainstorming meetings and creative getaways. You will be impressed by the beautiful and simple design.

ADOBE CREATIVE SUITE:

A bit pricey, but definitely worth the cost if you use apps like Photoshop and Illustrator enough. From editing photos to creating printable templates, web designs, and more, this is the go-to software for any professional creative type.

FINAL CUT PRO: If you like to shoot a lot of video and are ready to take your editing skills to the next level, Final Cut Pro is the software of choice.

GADGETS

LASER CUTTER: A machine that uses a small laser to cut or etch all kinds of materials ranging from wood to plastic to food. This is my personal favorite DIY gadget—the ideas of what you can create are endless!

CRICUT: An electronic cutting machine that can cut paper, vinyl, fabric, and more. It's like a laser cutter's kid sister.

AIRBRUSH: A handful of craft companies have recently created airbrushes that can be used with markers, makeup brushes, food pens, and more. Use them to get a gradient fade or a uniform coat of paint on whatever you are creating.

3D PRINTERS: There are now dozens of different 3D printing brands to choose from, but my favorite consumer printer is definitely the Makerbot. Pair it with the Makerbot 3D scanner to instantly print replicas of objects you may already have in your home, from wine glasses to kids' toys.

SUPPLIES

ARDUINO: An open-source electronics platform that lets artists and hobbyists create their own electronics gadgets. From robots to LED ball gowns and more, this is the go-to tool for hardware and software creatives alike.

RASPBERRY PI: A credit card–sized computer that can be attached to other electronics or even used as an SD card for storage. Hackers and tinkerers have been playing with Raspberry Pi for years, creating everything from baby monitors to smart microwaves. One of my favorite uses of it is in a product called the Egg-Bot, an Easter egg–decorating robot.

LED LIGHTS: As the price of LED lights, wires, and panels has gone down, they've become more affordable to use in your DIY projects. I've created a light-up umbrella, a laser-cut night-light, and even an LED cowboy hat that spells out my Twitter handle, @brit.

COLOR-BLOCKED PEGBOARD

MATERIALS	PEGBOARDS SPRAY PAINT (WHITE, GOLD, BLUE, MINT GREEN)
TOOLS	PAINTER'S TAPE

I love using pegboards to stay organized because it's so helpful to see all of the tools and supplies in your DIY arsenal. But pegboards don't have to be boring and beige like the ones in most people's garages. With a few cans of spray paint, you can easily make a pegboard organizer that doubles as wall art.

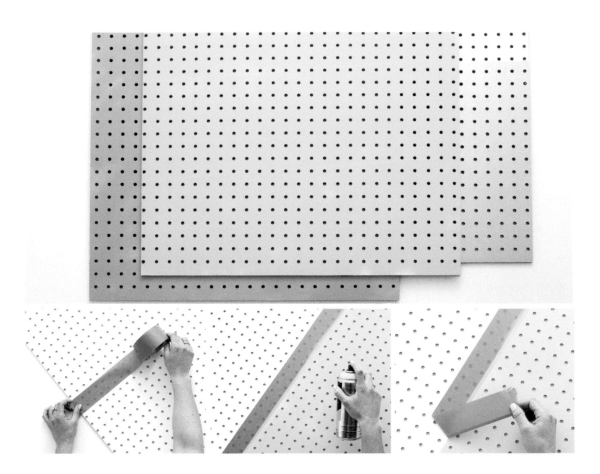

STEP 1: To make a pegboard more chic, spray-paint it white, then tape off a section at the bottom.

STEP 2: To create a "color-dipped" look, now spray-paint the pegboard with any color you like. I chose to "dip" my pegboards in gold, blue, and mint green.

STEP 3: Let the pegboard dry for 30 minutes or so, then peel off your tape.

How fun are these?

NOTES

PAINTED DESKTOP CADDY

MATERIALS	BLOCK OF WOOD
	WOOD STAIN
	WHITE PAINT

TOOLS	DRILL
	RAG
	PAINTER'S TAPE
	RULER
	PENCIL

I try to keep a minimalist workspace as much as I can, but I do love having essentials like colorful pens and pencils within arm's reach. Instead of going the Mason jar or painted tin can route, why not take things up a notch by creating this chic desktop caddy?

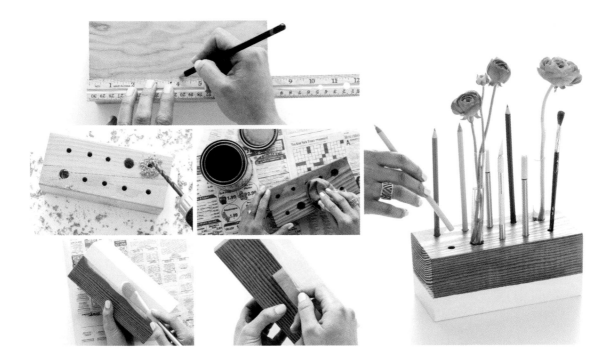

STEP 1: The key here is finding drill bits that will create holes in which pens and pencils can fit—or even a bud vase! Once you have those, use a pencil to mark where on your block you'll be drilling.

STEP 2: Drill those holes! We created two large holes and inserted a test tube to act as a bud vase. The rest fit pens, pencils, or paintbrushes nicely.

STEP 3: Use a rag to stain the wood block. Let it dry for an hour.

STEP 4: Place a piece of painter's tape around the block. Then dip the block in white paint by painting from the bottom up to the painter's tape. Let the block of wood dry for an hour.

STEP 5: Peel off the painter's tape.

STEP 6: Place all your favorite desktop essentials in the caddy, and you're good to go.

NOTES

CONCRETE PLANTER BOOKENDS

MATERIALS	VINYL LETTERS
	2 MILK CARTONS
	2 PLASTIC BOTTLES
	CONCRETE
	RED SPRAY PAINT
	SOIL AND SUCCULENTS

TOOLS	PLIERS

I might be obsessed with all things digital, but don't think that stops me from accumulating quite a collection of books, magazines, and other printed materials. So naturally, I've gotta have a stylish pair of bookends for adorning my desktop, bedside table, and mantel.

STEP 1: Cut off the tops of the two milk cartons. Milk cartons work best because the inside is covered in wax, making it easy to peel them off after the concrete has hardened.

STEP 2: Cut off the tops of the two plastic bottles. In terms of size, these should fit in the milk cartons with about an inch of space around each bottle.

STEP 3: Mix your concrete as directed on the package.

STEP 4: Pour concrete into one of your milk cartons.

STEP 5: Immediately press one of the plastic bottles into the milk carton filled with concrete.

STEP 6: Let harden overnight. Then use pliers to remove the plastic bottle.

STEP 7: Peel off the milk carton.

STEP 8: Now it's time to add some typography! I used vinyl letters to spell out three words we live by here at Brit + Co.

STEP 9: Spray-paint the entire planter with red spray paint—or any color you like! Let it dry for 30 minutes.

STEP 10: Peel off the letters to reveal your words.

STEP 11: Add soil and succulents, and you're done!

THE FUTURE WORKSPACE

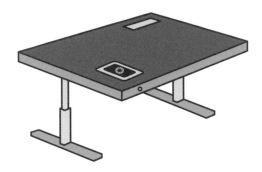

SMART DESK: If you work at any job that forces you to sit behind a computer, you'll probably admit that you aren't as active and healthy as you should be. But soon your desk may be able to better learn about you and your body, alerting you when it's time to stand up (and raising the desk so you can do so), calculating your calories burned throughout the day, and even offering a touchscreen surface, which may promote better ergonomics all around.

LASER CUTTER: Laser cutters aren't new by any means, but they are so expensive that most people don't know about them. And while the name suggests that a laser cutter can cut different sorts of materials using a heated laser, what the name  does not denote is that it can etch into the same materials as well. Once you experience this machine, your mind will explode with the possibilities for all the things you could create, from jewelry to clothing . . . even laser-etched food! A decent 16×12-inch laser bed will currently set you back about $10,000, but analysts are optimistic that this cost may fall in the future. Perhaps someday most homes will all have their own laser cutter, opening up a whole new world of creative projects.

3D PRINTER AND SCANNER: While 3D printers and scanners already exist, they are not as powerful, inexpensive, and mainstream as they will be one day. In the future, your home 3D printer will cost about as much as your home inkjet printer, yet it will be  able to produce objects from materials ranging from plastic to metal to ceramic to wood . . . perhaps even fabric (see page 288 on the Future Closet). And don't forget to pair your printer with a scanner, which can scan any object and convert the photograph into a 3D design file for you to reprint or modify however you want.

CNC MILL: If a 3D printer's functionality can be referred to as "additive manufacturing" (because the layers of material are essentially "adding" up one over the other), then a CNC mill's functionality is best described as "subtractive 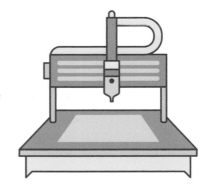 manufacturing." Place a metal block of aluminum inside a CNC machine and it starts whittling away at the block until it is shaped to the design that the machine has been programmed to create. CNC mills have been around for ages, but they are only now coming out in forms that are small enough to fit on your desk or countertop but powerful enough to cut through the strongest of materials.

INTERACTIVE WHITEBOARDS:

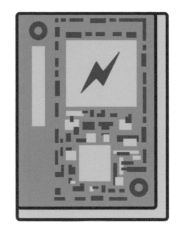

Imagine that drawings and text on your chalkboards and whiteboards will soon be digitally recorded . . . as you are drawing or writing on the boards. Not only that, but these interactive boards will also be able to connect to Wi-Fi, making it easy for your creative pals on the other side of the world to draw alongside you. The implications for collaborative learning, brainstorming, and art are tremendous.

NOTES

G Y M

Believe it or not, fitness is at an all-time technology high today. There are so many new, more practical ways to work out from home, thanks to many different apps, gadgets, and services that are now here to help. Couple that with the fact that people around the world are taking a deeper interest in their bodies and you've got an explosion of new ways to stay healthy and fit.

Over the years, my own fitness regimen has included a hodgepodge of routines. I've tried gyms, personal trainers, self-training, and almost every type of fitness class. My husband tells people that I'm one of the "crazies" who actually enjoys working out. And while that is not always true (there are definitely days when I begrudge having to yank myself out of bed and into my workout spandex), I have found out how to trick myself into wanting to get (and stay) fit. Yes, I said "trick." Unless you really are crazy, your body is likely to initially reject the pain you give it with a hard workout. So you have to find ways to inflict that pain on yourself without realizing it's so . . . um . . . painful. These are a few of the things that work for me, and hopefully they'll work for you too. We're in this together, sister!

Heart Rate 101

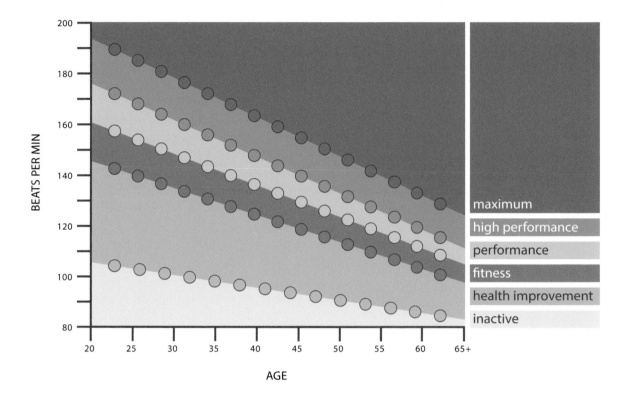

Most people have a resting heart rate between 60 and 90 beats per minute. That's a pretty wide variance, and so not all exercises have the same impact on every person. Everyone should know their resting and maximum heart rates in order to determine the fitness and cardio level they want to achieve for maximum endurance and calorie burn.

CALCULATIONS TO KNOW

RESTING VS. MAXIMUM HEART RATE

Here's the formula: 220 minus your age equals your maximum heart rate. Your best workout range is 50%–85% of your max heart rate. To find your heart rate, just count your pulse for 10 seconds at your wrist or neck, then multiply by 6.

WAIST-TO-HIP RATIO

Your WHR is your waist size in inches divided by your hip size in inches. For women, if your WHR is 0.80 or less, you are a "pear." If your WHR is greater than 0.80, you are an "apple." For men, a WHR of greater than 0.90 means that you not only are an apple but are also at increased risk for heart disease. (See page 252 to get a better understanding of your body shape and how to dress for it.)

HYDRATION PER DAY

Are you drinking enough water? Confession: I'm usually not. Water is the basis of our hydration and health, and though it's not always the preferred beverage for most people, it's essential to make sure you are hitting your daily targets. To find out exactly how much you need, just use this handy formula: your weight in pounds divided by two equals the number of ounces you should be drinking. So a 120-pound woman should be drinking approximately 60 ounces, or nearly 8 cups per day.

INTERVALS VS. LONG DISTANCE

It's been proven that high-intensity interval training (often abbreviated to HIIT) is a much more effective and efficient workout than endurance training. By increasing your heart rate in intervals, you are forcing your heart to work harder as it spikes, then drops, every minute or two. Over time, you also burn more calories this way. If you often run on a treadmill and want to make your workout much less boring, consider my favorite interval workout. Depending on how hard you work, it can scorch nearly 500 calories in about 30 minutes!

BRIT'S GO-TO INTERVAL WORKOUT

MINUTE	INCLINE	SPEED
0–1	1	5, 6, or 7
1–2	3	5, 6, or 7
2–3	5	5, 6, or 7
3–4	0	4
4–14	0	Start at 5.0, then increase by 0.5 every minute
14–15	0	4
15–16	5	4
16–17	10	4
17–18	12	4
18–19	0	4
19–20	0	5, 6, or 7
20–21	0	8, 9, or 10
21–22	0	4
22–23	0	5, 6, or 7
23–24	0	8, 9, or 10
24–25	0	4
25–26	0	5, 6, or 7
26–27	0	8, 9, or 10
27–30	0	4

COMMON DIETS

These days everyone has a different reason for the way they eat. Here are today's most common diets.

VEGAN

The vegan dieter eats nothing that is animal based, including all meats, eggs, dairy, and honey.

VEGETARIAN

The majority of vegetarians choose a diet that limits all animal-based foods except for eggs, dairy, and honey.

PALEO

The paleo dieter eats like a caveman. No really! The rule of this diet is that "if a caveman couldn't eat it, neither can you." This means you can eat anything that you could hunt or find. The possibilities range from meats and fish to nuts, veggies, and seeds.

LOW-CARB

There's no consensus on what constitutes a low-carbohydrate diet, but many say that low-carb dieters should keep their carbs under 100 grams per day in order to qualify. Beware of the carbs found in many foods other than bread and pastas—they lie hidden in nearly everything! Google the phrase "carb chart" to browse websites that list the best and worst offenders.

LOW-FAT

Like the low-carb diet, there's a lot of mixed opinions about what constitutes a low-fat diet, although most agree that having fat be between 15% and 30% of your daily caloric intake would qualify.

LOW-CALORIE

Probably the most popular diet among Westerners, the low-calorie diet is all about staying below a certain caloric benchmark that you set for yourself, with the understanding that losing a pound of fat requires cutting 3,500 calories from your diet.

RAW FOOD

The raw food dieter consumes only food and drinks that are unprocessed, completely plant-based, and completely organic. You may remember Alicia Silverstone being at the vanguard of this diet trend over the last few years.

Tips from the Co:

BEST YOUTUBE WORKOUT CHANNELS

It's easier than ever to work out at home these days, thanks in part to YouTube. Here are some of the best YouTube channels that offer full workouts you can do in your home gym or even in your living room. I'm a personal fan of FitnessBlender and even spin up a few of their videos in my hotel room whenever I'm traveling and can't get to a good gym. The others on this list were submitted by the Brit + Co community across some of our social network channels.

1. FitnessBlender

2. Blogilates

3. Caroline Fitness

4. ToneItUp

5. CharlieJames1975

6. arFit

Measuring tape

Jump rope

Dumbbells

Mat

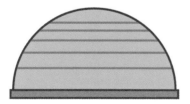

Bosu ball

Foam roller

Pro Tip:
*If you're a
biker, cuff your
bracelet around
your ankle to
make sure the
tracker is able
to include your
mad cycling
skills in your
day's activity.*

ACTIVITY TRACKERS: There's now an endless variety of bracelets and wearables that can track how much you are moving every day. These tracking devices use pedometers and altimeters to understand your activity, then convert those numbers into your average amount of calories burned throughout the day.

1350 STEPS

DIET TRACKERS: If the ultimate way to a healthy weight is by "moving more and eating less" (something my doctor always told me), then a diet-tracking app is a necessity when combined with your fitness tracker. Apps like MyFitnessPal and other nutrition counters are available in your phone's app store and aid you in recording all of the foods and drinks you consume each day, making it easier to stay on track with your diet goals.

S'WELL BOTTLE: Okay, so this isn't technically a "gadget," but it does have some high-tech qualities that other water bottles and drinking thermoses do not. It can keep cold drinks cold for up to 24 hours and hot drinks hot for up to 12 hours. Bonus: No condensation occurs on these bottles, so you never have to worry about wet hands.

VESSYL: By far the coolest new advance in nutrition technology, the Vessyl is a thermos with sensors that can give you nutritional information on whatever is inside it. From ounces to calories, sugars,

proteins, and more, you will never second-guess how good (or bad) for you your beverages are. Soon you may even be able to track the same nutritional information for your food using a special fork with similar embedded sensor technology.

MOVES: If wearable devices aren't your thing, then consider downloading the Moves app. On the assumption that you carry your phone with you everywhere, it takes advantage of your phone's native features like GPS and an accelerometer to give you an effortless way to track how much you walk, run, cycle, or drive each day.

RUNNING AND CYCLING TRACKERS: As a frequent runner, I always like to improve my mile times and distances. Apps like Nike+ and Strava are my favorite options for recording my runs. You can even share your run (or ride) to your social network once it's completed to get kudos from your friends on a workout well done.

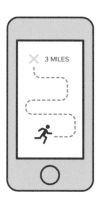

SEVEN-MINUTE WORKOUT: The American College of Sports Medicine's *Health and Fitness Journal* was the first to promote the idea that a high-intensity seven-minute workout is the minimum needed to get the same fitness benefits of a prolonged endurance workout. Using nothing but your body weight, this app guides you through the workout routine from the comfort of your own home.

RISE: Whether or not you're overweight, it's always a good idea to seek counsel from a nutritionist if you're interested in a healthier diet. Rise is an app that connects you with a preapproved community of professional nutritionists who can help advise you and monitor your diet on a daily basis through forums like text messaging and digital video.

WELLNESSFX: If you've ever wondered how your body *really* works, look no further than WellnessFX, a diagnostic testing service that offers a streamlined visualization of your overall health. You'll be asked to get a quick blood draw at a local lab. Results are sent to you just days later and show you everything from hormonal imbalances to disease risks. You'll be given the opportunity to get additional insights about your health from licensed medical practitioners.

SMART SCALES: It's been proven that those who monitor their weight generally have less weight fluctuation overall. Smart scales like the Fitbit Aria and Withings scales can not only measure your weight but detect your body mass index and body fat percentage. The results are documented to an online account and mobile app where you can browse them and track changes over time.

SMART CARDIO MACHINES: Your treadmill is getting as smart as your phone. Many cardio machines are now being built on top of platforms like Android, which, when connected to the Internet, can not only personalize your workouts for you but display high-resolution Google Street View imagery to make it feel like you are running through foreign cities or on famous beaches. Some machines even let you connect to other runners to virtually compete in races.

YOGA MAT CARRYING STRAP

MATERIALS	1½-INCH D-RINGS
	1¼-INCH YARDS THICK FABRIC

TOOLS	SEWING PINS
	SEWING MACHINE
	FABRIC SCISSORS

Love getting your yoga on? Then you could probably use this easy-to-make carrying strap! In this project, I'll show you how to make your own basic strap that can be adjusted to fit any yoga mat. You can even use the same method to create a strap for a camping mattress, picnic blanket, or rug—though I'm not sure why you'd need to carry a rug around town. This project is also a great Sewing 101 tutorial for those of you who never got instruction from your mom or home ec teacher.

STEP 1: Cut three strips of fabric. One will be the shoulder strap, and two will be belt-like straps that wrap around your yoga mat. The shoulder strap should be 38 inches long by 3 inches wide—based on 1½-inch D-rings.

STEP 2: To create the mat straps, measure the circumference of your yoga mat when it is rolled up. Add 6 inches and cut your fabric to that measurement by 3 inches wide. For my strap, the measurement was 19 inches by 3 inches.

STEP 3: Fold each piece in half lengthwise, with the inside of the fabric facing out. Iron and sew along the edge of each strap.

STEP 4: Turn all three straps inside out, so that the front fabric is facing the right way. Iron them!

STEP 5: Add D-rings to the end of the shorter mat straps by folding the ends of the straps through the rings and sewing them into place. You will need two D-rings on each strap, and there should be about an inch of fabric folded over the rings. Make sure to sew a proper hem by folding the edge twice. Now hem the other end of these straps. Do this with both mat straps.

STEP 6: Lay one of your D-ring straps flat and then place the longer strap perpendicular to the D-ring strap and right in the middle.

STEP 7: Take the long strap and fold the edge over twice. Then sew that piece to the shorter strap. Repeat the same steps with your other mat strap, and you're done!

STEP 8: Strap those straps right onto your yoga mat.

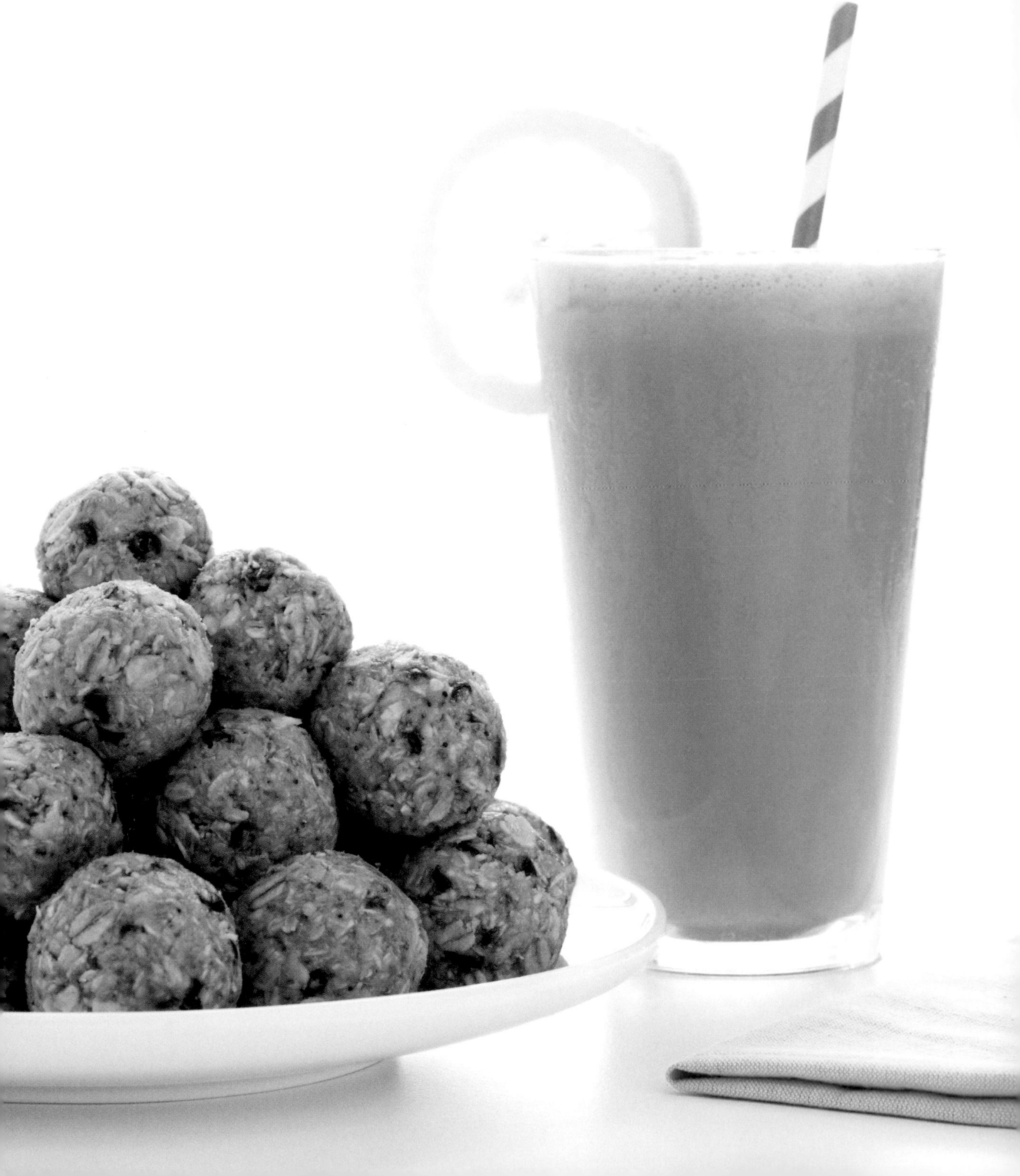

BRIT'S DAILY GREEN SMOOTHIE

Kick off your morning with a blast of veggies, courtesy of this delicious—yes, delicious—green smoothie. I drink this every day and feel it gives me not only a ton of nutrients but also a burst of energy.

INGREDIENTS

2 large kale leaves, stems removed

2 large romaine leaves

2 cups spinach (about two handfuls)

1 stalk celery, roughly chopped

2 cups milk (regular, soy, or almond works great)

1 large handful of berries or your fruit of choice
(a banana works great too)

3 tablespoons lemon juice

2 cups water

Ice as needed

INSTRUCTIONS

Blend together all ingredients in a powerful blender
(a Vitamix is my favorite for this drink) until smooth, adding
ice until desired temperature and consistency are reached.
Makes enough for three to four 12-ounce servings.
Refrigerate whatever is unused for up to three days.

POWER-PACKED ENERGY BALLS

These are a great protein-packed snack to make ahead of time and keep in the fridge so you can grab them on the go. I also like to keep a couple of these in my purse to chow down on after working out at the gym.

INGREDIENTS

1 cup oats

1 cup unsweetened coconut flakes

¼ cup ground flaxseed

½ cup peanut or almond butter

¼ cup Medjool dates, chopped

2 tablespoons honey or agave nectar

½ cup mini chocolate chips

3 tablespoons chia seeds

1 teaspoon vanilla

INSTRUCTIONS

Mix all ingredients together in a large bowl. Divide into tablespoon-sized portions and roll into balls. Refrigerate or freeze until ready to serve.

NOTES

THE FUTURE GYM

SMART HEADPHONES: If you work out with headphones like I do, then you know how annoying it is to deal with cords swinging back and forth. New headphones like Dash are solving this problem by becoming wireless.

But that's not all. These headphones can also detect your heart rate and thus calories burned, making them a perfect fitness accessory for any workout.

NUTRITION TRACKING:

Sensor technology is getting good enough (and small enough) to fit inside areas as tiny as the tip of a fork, so that it may not be long before our

utensils are telling us the nutritional status (calories, fats, sugars) of what we're eating and drinking. Unlike checking a nutrition label on a package of food, these sensors will be able to detect exactly how much you are consuming, based on the weight of the object on your plate or fork. That will give us more precise information on exactly what is going into our bodies each day.

SMART SPORTS EQUIPMENT:

Turns out, the "Internet of Things" really does mean all things. Many sporting goods products, ranging from basketballs to tennis rackets, now have  sensors inside of them that can give you feedback on your game, from how hard you hit the ball to the number of baskets you made. There are even special running shoes that can track total miles ran. Will the athletes of the future be even better than today given all of the data they'll have as they train?

PERSONALIZED MEDICINE: Because so many new technologies will soon exist that can extract all kinds of information about our health, diet, and fitness levels, in the not-too-distant future it will be easier for doctors to  treat us more specifically. Isn't it crazy that all adults, no matter our size, shape, or medical past, are still told to take the same amount of over-the-counter medications? In the future, we'll have personalized vitamins and medications that are specifically formulated to treat our bodies.

PERFORMANCE WEAR: As discussed on page 241, new smart materials like graphene are getting embedded into everything from our mattresses to our clothing. When embedded into our gym clothes, shoes, and  accessories, we'll be able to track our performance simply by the objects we're wearing—no fancy fitness tracking bracelets required.

9

BACK PORCH

At Brit + Co, the "Co" is a big part of who we are. It stands for "Community," and as you have seen throughout this book, it's a community full of many creative and intelligent minds. Creativity is a trait that everyone is born with, and it's for that reason that I always like to feature some of the coolest ideas and tips from the crowd. This chapter is full of projects submitted from our community of both professional and hobbyist chefs, makers, and DIYers. I hope you enjoy them as much as I do.

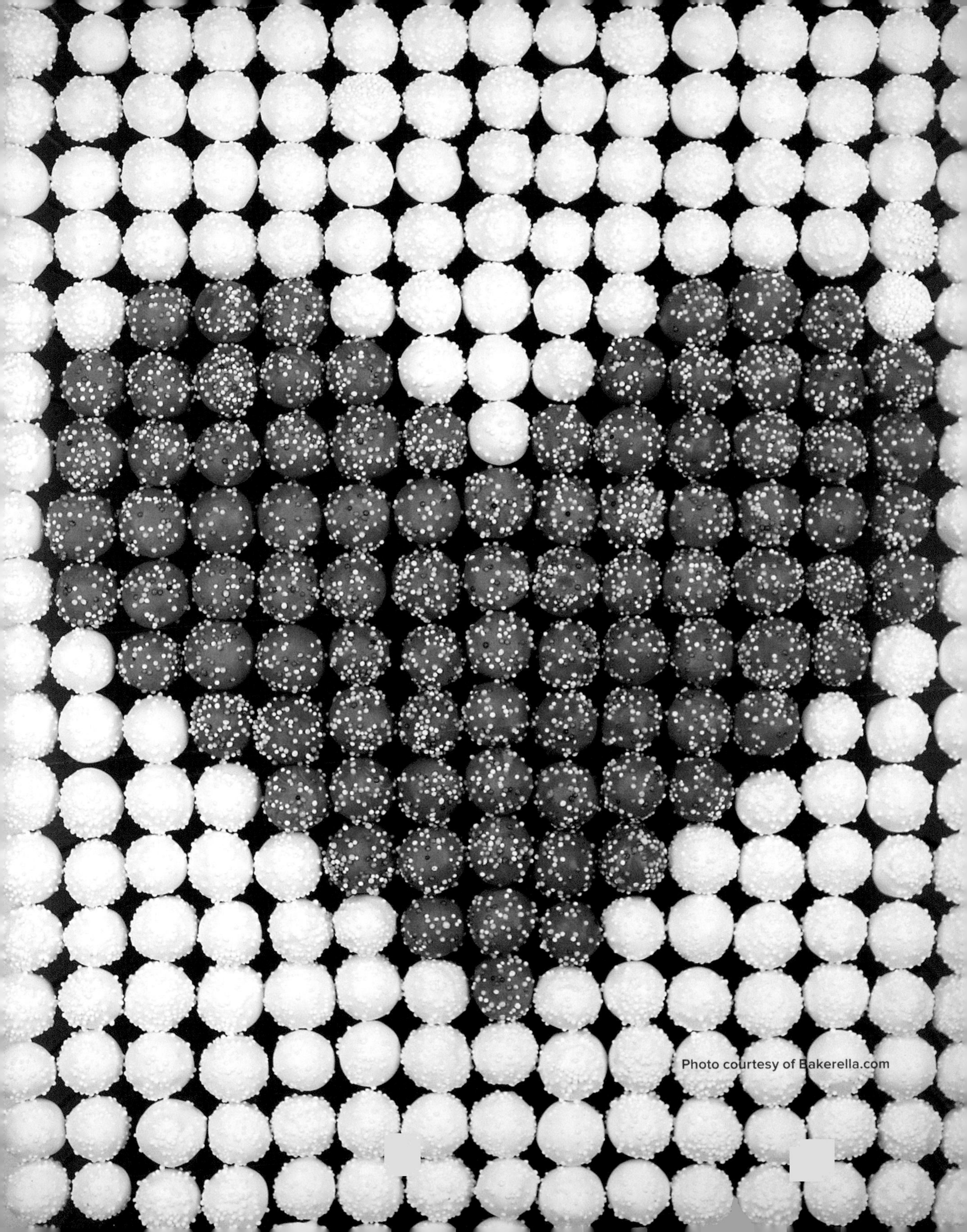

Photo courtesy of Bakerella.com

CAKE POPS MOSAIC

BY ANGIE DUDLEY (AKA BAKERELLA)

ANGIE DUDLEY is the creator of cake pops and author of the *New York Times* best-seller *Cake Pops* by Bakerella. On her website, www.bakerella .com, Angie chronicles her adventures in baking and explores fun recipes, desserts, and decorating while inspiring others to do the same.

Photo courtesy of Bakerella.com

SUPPLIES AND INGREDIENTS FOR THE BASIC CAKE POP RECIPE

1 box cake mix (cook as directed on the box for a 13×9-inch cake)

1 can frosting (16 ounces)

Wax paper

Pink and white candy melts (1-pound package)

White and multicolored nonpareil sprinkles

Toothpicks

INSTRUCTIONS

STEP 1: After the cake is cooked and cooled completely, crumble it into a large bowl.

STEP 2: Mix thoroughly with one can of frosting. (I used the back of a large spoon, but it may be easier to use your fingers to mix it all together. Be warned: it will get messy. Also, you may not need the entire can of frosting, so start out by using almost the entire can and add more if you need to.)

STEP 3: Roll into tiny cake balls. You can use the circles on the template (see step 13) as a guide for making them the right size. They should be slightly smaller than the circle so that when you add the coating they still fit together nicely.

STEP 4: Keep rolling and rolling until you have enough cake balls.

STEP 5: Chill cake balls in the refrigerator for 30 to 45 minutes.

STEP 6: Dip a toothpick into the melted coating and then insert it into a chilled cake ball.

STEP 7: Dip the entire cake pop into the coating and then sprinkle with nonpareils, which are tiny enough for these tiny treats.

STEP 8: Place the cake pop in Styrofoam to dry.

STEP 9: Use multicolored nonpareils for the second candy coating color.

STEP 10: When all the pops are done, prepare your display.

STEP 11: Wrap a 12 × 18-inch or 12 × 20-inch sheet of Styrofoam with paper. I used the 19 × 25-inch single sheets you can purchase at a craft store. You could also use wrapping paper.

STEP 12: Packing tape works best on the Styrofoam to tape down the paper.

STEP 13: Print out the template provided on bakerella.com and center on an 11 × 17-inch sheet of paper. The design is created for a 12 × 18-inch surface area, but it is set up on 11 × 17-inch paper, since that is a standard size to print. You'll notice that some of the circles on the template are getting cropped off when they print, but that's okay—you'll have enough information to figure out where the pops on the perimeter should go. I hope that makes sense.

STEP 14: Tape the template down temporarily and use a safety pin to poke holes in the paper.

STEP 15: Remove the template and start arranging the cake pops using the template as a guide. Start in the middle and work your way out from the center because, more than likely, some of your pops will be bigger than you think. If you start at one end, working left to right, they will start to tilt too much to make room as you place them in position. But if you start in the center, they will angle out equally all the way around.

Photos courtesy of Bakerella.com

COLORED PENCIL CANDLES

BY VICTORIA HUDGINS

VICTORIA HUDGINS is the author of the popular lifestyle blog A Subtle Revelry, a craft and foodie site filled with simple ideas for finding revelry in the everyday—because every day deserves a party! Visit her website at www.asubtlerevelry.com.

Photo courtesy of Victoria Hudgins, creator of A Subtle Revelry

Running short on candles? Or just want to add a more colorful and creative spin to the top of your next cake? Turns out, colored pencils have enough wax in their tips to stay lit for up to two minutes. Try it at your next event to start a conversation and turn heads.

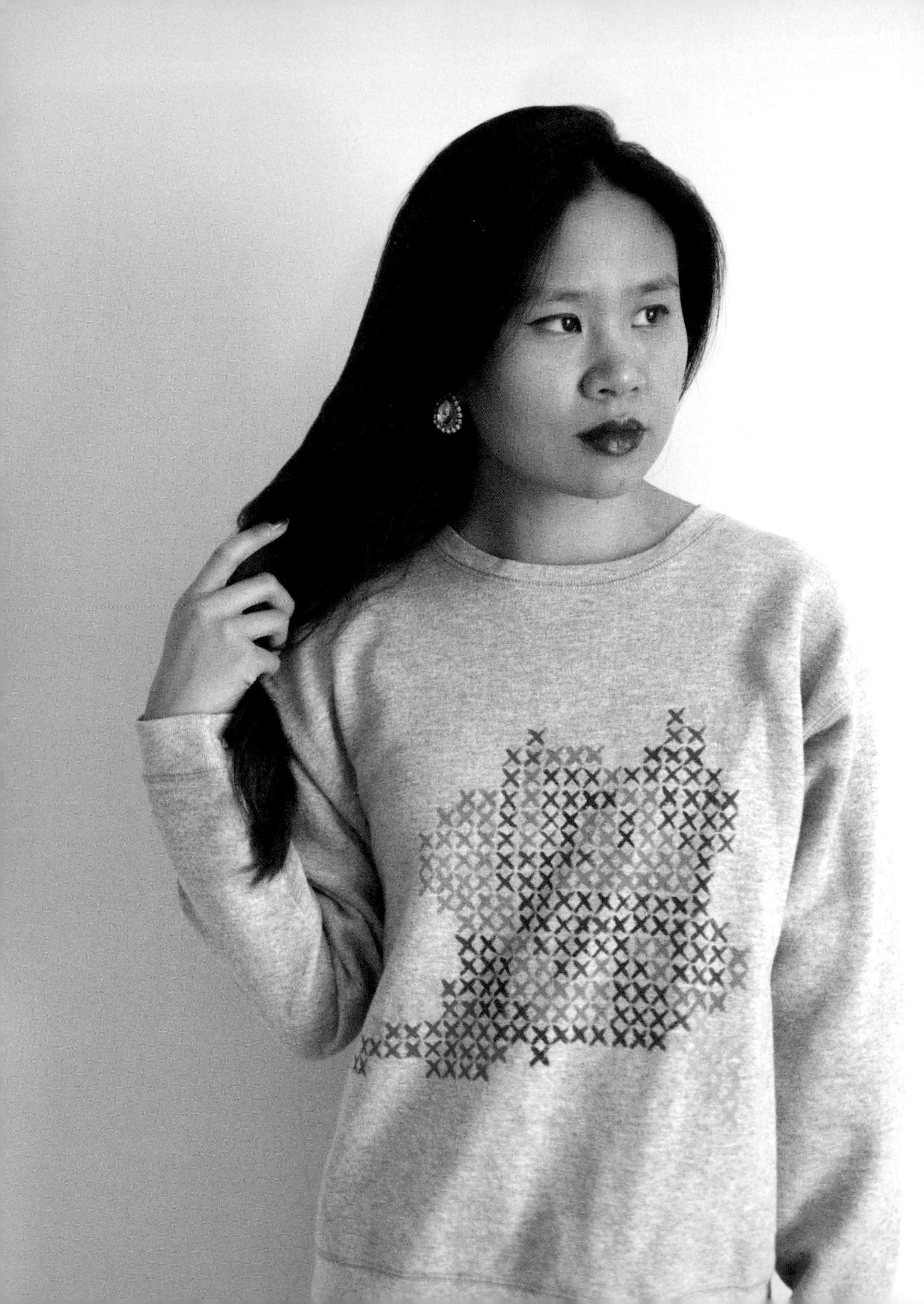

Photo courtesy of Kirsten Nunez

FAUX CROSS-STITCHED SWEATSHIRT

BY KIRSTEN NUNEZ

Based in New York, **KIRSTEN NUNEZ** is an author, crafty lady, and food enthusiast at www.Studs-and-Pearls.com. Her blog features edgy DIY fashion tutorials, home decor projects, and innovative recipes. Since 2010, her work has received coverage in a variety of media outlets, ranging from CNN Living to international magazines.

Photo courtesy of Kirsten Nunez

SUPPLIES

Fabric paint (or acrylic paint and fabric medium) in dark pink/red, pink, light pink, green, and mint green

Sweatshirt

Paintbrush

Highlighter

Marker

Masking tape

Ruler and measuring tape

Printed faux cross-stitch rose template

COLOR KEY

A Red/dark pink

B Pink

C Light pink

D Green

E Mint green

```
                              D E E
                  D               D D E
              D D  C L L      B B B
            D  C B B B  C B B  B B B
        C C  B C B  B A A  C C A B B B
      C C C  B C  B A  C A  C C A A C A B B
      C L C  L B A  C A C L  A C C A B B
      C L C  L B B A B B  C C C C C A
      C L L  C B B A  L C C C C C C B
        C C  L C A A  B A A  B B A B
        C C C A A A B B A A A  B B B
          B A  C C B B A A  A C C B B B  C
          B B A L C B B C A A C B  B B C
        E D B B A C C  L C C A B B C C C
      E  E  D D B B A C  L C B B B E
    E D  D D D D D  B B A  B B B  B B E E  E E
  D D D  D D D D D D  D   A               E E E
D D          D D  D D                       E E E
                                              E
```

INSTRUCTIONS

STEP 1: After printing out the template, create a 16 × 16-inch square with the highlighter. The entire pattern will not be included in this square; the leftover "stitches" can be easily added once most of the rose is painted.

STEP 2: Each square—or letter—on the graph paper represents one half-inch "stitch," or one painted "x." Therefore, each blank square on the graph paper will be a space of half an inch on your sweatshirt. Each "x" will also measure half an inch when painted.

STEP 3: With masking tape, re-create the highlighted square on your sweatshirt. The actual perimeter of the inside square should be 8 × 8 inches. (The 8 inches on each side is calculated from the 16 half-inch squares.)

STEP 4: Along the side, add a mark every half inch (each row of squares or stitches).

STEP 5: Along the top, add a mark (represented by the first four blank squares) to indicate the placement of your first stitch. Also mark the placement of your last stitch.

STEP 6: Line up your ruler along the first horizontal mark. Add the first stitch, using the top mark as a guide.

STEP 7: Continue according to the template.

STEP 8: When you have completed a row, cross it out on the template to avoid confusion.

STEP 9: Once the first row is done, move your ruler down half an inch and continue adding stitches.

STEP 10: Repeat until the entire pattern is completed.

STEP 11: If you mess up, don't worry! The pattern is super forgiving and it won't show in the whole grand scheme of things. I highly recommend simply leaving a mistake instead of trying to fix it.

STEP 12: Section by section, remove the tape and add any of the extra stitches outside of the initial perimeter. Use the existing stitches as a guide.

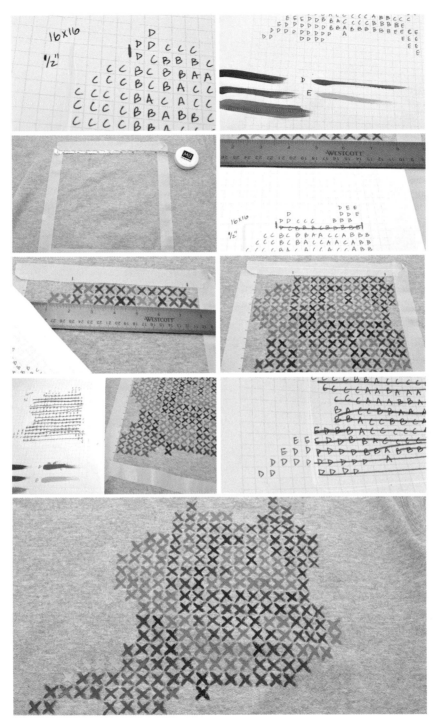

Photos courtesy of Kirsten Nunez

Concept, photography, and styling by Brittini Mehlhoff of Paper & Stitch.
Modeling by Amanda Toman.

FLORAL PENDANT LIGHT

BY BRITTNI MEHLHOFF

BRITTNI MEHLHOFF is an editor and craft stylist who enjoys making the ordinary extraordinary with modern DIY projects, ranging from watercolor meringues and ombre doughnuts to floating geometric flower wreaths and faux copper planters. Her DIY lifestyle blog, Paper & Stitch, has been named one of the 12 most beautiful creative blogs on the Internet by Bridgette.de.

Photo by Sarahdipity

MATERIALS

MAIN FLOWERS: dahlias (in dark red, burgundy, and purple), mini calla lilies (in burgundy), and purple veronica filler: wax flowers, thistle eryngium Orion, scabiosa pods, and privet berries

GREENERY: viburnum berries, dusty miller, and green pittosporum

LIGHT KIT: pendant cord and lightbulb

Large wire basket with a hole at the top that your light kit will fit through

Floral tape

Floral wire (two gauges—one thin and one thick/heavy-duty)

Scissors

Wire cutters (optional—for the thicker-gauge wire)

Before you get started, let's talk about flower care. Dahlias are sensitive to dirty water, so if you're keeping them in a vase or bucket for a prolonged period, just make sure to recut them and replace the water daily. Mini callas only need one to one and a half inches of water; too much water is actually not good for callas—it can make the stems turn mushy too quickly. For everything else, cut at least one inch off each stem and place the flowers in three to four inches of room-temperature water. Let everything hydrate for at least three to four hours before you start working with them.

INSTRUCTIONS

STEP 1: First things first: flip your basket over so the bottom is facing up. This is the framework for your pendant lampshade. Now you're ready to begin. You'll want to start with the greenery (like green pittosporum) as your base. Cut off decent-size sprigs (six to ten inches) from a larger branch and begin attaching them to the wire basket with floral wire. You can also weave some of the pieces in and out of the basket for extra security. For heavy stems or branches, use the heavy-gauge wire. Start weaving some of the other greenery into the frame at this time as well (like viburnum berries).

STEP 2: Once the basket has been fairly well covered with the greenery all the way around (you don't have to fill in every hole because there are plenty of flowers still to add—this is just the start), add a few filler flowers, like wax flowers, to fill in some of the gaps. Secure them with wire just as you did with the greenery. You can also add some sprigs of dusty miller around the base at this time.

STEP 3: Now that the lampshade is starting to fill out a little bit, it's time to start adding the really cool flowers, like mini calla lilies, dahlias, and purple veronica. Cut the stems fairly short (leave about five to six inches) and start weaving them

into the shade, securing with wire as you go. Before securing flowers in certain spots, I would just kind of push the stem through the basket and then step back to see if it looks good. If you're happy with it, secure it with wire. If not, move it to another spot and look at it from a distance again before securing it.

STEP 4: Once most of the main flowers have been added, you can add some of the smaller fillers to round everything out. The thistle, berries, and scabiosa pods are perfect for this part. Cut the stems down to five to six inches before adding them, just like the others. *Note:* If you need to cover any additional areas but find you have run out of flowers, add greenery like dusty miller a couple of leaves at a time to fill in holes that have gone unnoticed. (I wouldn't recommend adding a whole stem at once—that's a lot of leaves.)

STEP 5: Once you're happy with the arrangement, it's time to add the light kit. As luck would have it, my light fit perfectly into the hole at the top of the wire basket. Then I screwed in the bottom piece of the light kit from underneath, and it was perfectly secure. Add a lightbulb and you are ready to shine some light on your fresh flower masterpiece.

Concept, photography, and styling by Brittini Mehlhoff of Paper & Stitch. Modeling by Amanda Toman.

IKEA HACK FOR WOODEN SHELVES

BY ASHLEY ROSE

Photo courtesy of Ashley Rose
of Sugar & Cloth. www.sugarandcloth.com

ASHLEY ROSE is the editor and founder of Sugar & Cloth, a blog filled with everything you need for DIY-inspired living. You can see her work in places such as *O, The Oprah Magazine, Martha Stewart Living, Uppercase, HGTV,* and *Apartment Therapy.* Ashley's blog was also named a "Top 10 DIY Blog" by *Better Homes & Gardens.*

MATERIALS

Wood stain in preferred colors (a medium brown works best)

Paintbrush

EKBY shelving brackets

Untreated wooden shelves

Hand towel

INSTRUCTIONS

STEP 1: Using random tools and utensils, like screws, a hammer, sandpaper, or punches, begin marking and scraping the unfinished wood pieces. Use the sandpaper to round out the edges a bit and smooth out any major bumps caused from distressing the wood.

STEP 2: Once the wood is distressed as much as you'd like it to be, brush stain onto the wood, allowing it to dry to the touch in between coats. Apply the second coat only in certain areas, and use the hand towel to blend the edges of the second coat into the first. This will make certain spots a bit darker than others—the variety of colors will give the shelves a reclaimed-wood effect—and make the distressed areas look more interesting. You can also use the IKEA clear glaze finish to seal the wood from water.

STEP 3: Once the stain has dried completely, install the EKBY shelving ends according to the instructions on the package. You'll definitely want an extra set of hands for this part!

STEP 4: Now that your shelves are installed, decorate them with as many pretties as you'd like, and you've got yourself custom distressed wooden shelves for a fraction of the cost!

WOODEN JEWELRY DISPLAY CASE

BY ZANDRA ZURAW
AND KAREN JUNE GRANT

KAREN JUNE GRANT and **ZANDRA ZURAW** are the creators behind Little Yellow Couch, a lifestyle and design blog organized around a theme that changes monthly. For them, building a meaningful life and creating a home that reflects that life are what defines them as "modern homemakers."

Photo courtesy of Little Yellow Couch

MATERIALS

Wooden crates (look for these at garage sales or flea markets)

Half-inch cup hooks (find them at your local hardware store)

TOOLS

Electric drill

$\frac{1}{16}$-inch drill bit

Small pliers

INSTRUCTIONS

STEP 1: Predrill your holes at even intervals. (We spaced ours about 1¾ inches apart, offsetting a second row farther back and another set on top of the crate for longer necklaces.)

STEP 2: Using pliers, screw the cup hooks into the predrilled holes.

STEP 3: Hang and enjoy your jewelry!

Thanks to Airbnb for teaming up with
us to find the perfect photo location for
each chapter of this book. The homes
you see featured throughout this book are
Airbnb listings hand-selected as part of our partnership.
Both companies believe in helping the world live more creatively,
from unique experiences while traveling, to inspiring moments made in the home.

airbnb

Acknowledgments

To everyone who made this book possible, from our incredible community of Brit + Co fans, bloggers, partners, and makers to the insanely talented team that I get to work with on a daily basis. Special high-fives to those of you who spent hours on end helping to make this book as beautiful, informative, and entertaining as it turned out to be.

To my friends, new and old, who have supported me throughout this crazy entrepreneurial journey of starting Brit + Co. You have been there for me during the highs and lows, text messages and phone calls, stressed-out days and celebratory milestones. I appreciate you letting me ramble on and on about all of my grand ideas as you listen patiently with a smile on your face.

To my parents, for raising me with a respect for both the arts and sciences and a drive to succeed in the workplace. I'm especially grateful for your openness to let me explore the Internet at such an early age (nine). And for that cell phone you purchased for me when I turned thirteen, automatically making me the "cool tech girl" among all of my middle school friends. I look back and remember those years as the beginning of my curiosity and fascination with technology.

To my son, Ansel, for not making me overly tired or sick throughout my pregnancy, leaving me with enough energy to write this book and take (God knows how many) photos with a genuine smile on my face. Thank you also for teaching me what unconditional love feels like. My heart has never melted so much as the day you first smiled at me. P.S.: You are hidden in my belly on the cover!

To my husband, Dave, my partner in life, love, and business. You have been a role model for me ever since the day I met you. I wake up every day inspired by your intelligence, ideas, and passion to change the world. You have supported me throughout the valleys and the mountains (some literal), always encouraging me to follow my heart. I especially appreciate you for being the beta tester of my food inventions and new product ideas, and for (usually) laughing at all of my corny jokes. You are the Jay-Z to my Beyoncé.

Finally, to every woman out there who has had the realization that they are creative and talented enough to master life in the workplace and in the home. You are the force that will drive the next generation of women to achieve, inspire, and innovate, wherever they choose to lay their ground.

Resources

ENTRYWAY

1 **72% DOWNLOADED AT LEAST ONE APP:** http://thecurvereport.com/article/inter-app-tivity/

5 **"FORTY-TWO PERCENT OF GEN X AND GENY Y":** http://thecurvereport.com/article/counter-culture/

23 **"IS NOT ONLY EXPENSIVE AND INCONVENIENT":** http://pdfpiw.uspto .gov/.piw?Docid= 1931892&idkey=NONE&homeurl=http%3A%2F%2Fpatft%2Fnetahtml%2FPTO%2Fpatimg.htm

25 **BY 1968, ROUGHLY 25% OF HOUSEHOLDS:** http://en.wikipedia.org/wiki/Microwave_oven

CHAPTER 1: KITCHEN

70 **COMMON COOKING TERMS:** Roberta Larson Duyff, *Food Nutrition, and Wellness* (Woodland Hills, CA: Glencoe/McGraw-Hill 2003)

CHAPTER 4: BEDROOM

218 **ONCE YOU'RE IN A RELATIONSHIP, ODDS ARE:** http://metro.co.uk/2013/08/21/men-wash-their-sheets-four-times-a-year-new-survey-claims-3933231/

CHAPTER 5: CLOSET

251 **THE HOURGLASS IS NORMALLY ACCEPTED:** http://www.calculator.net/body-type-calculator .html

CHAPTER 7: WORKSPACE

335 **AND IF YOU'RE LIKE 9.5% OF THE COUNTRY:** http://www.census.gov/prod/2012pubs/ p70-132.pdf

Index